RICH BROTT

30 Biblical Principles for Managing Your Money

Insights That Will Set You Free!

Published by
ABC Book Publishing

AbcBookPublishing.com
Printed in U.S.A.

30 Biblical Principles for Managing Your Money:
Insights That Will Set You Free!

10 Digit ISBN: 1-60185-012-3
13 Digit ISBN (EAN): 978-1-60185-012-6
Cover and Interior Text Design by AliceLove@att.net

First Edition, January 2008

About the Author

Rich Brott holds a Bachelor of Science degree in Business and Economics and a Master of Business Administration.

Rich has served in an executive position with some very successful businesses. He has functioned on the board of directors for churches, businesses, and charities and served on a college advisory board.

He has authored over twenty books:

- *5 Simple Keys to Financial Freedom*
- *10 Life-Changing Attitudes That Will Make You a Financial Success*
- *15 Biblical Responsibilities Leading to Financial Wisdom*
- *30 Biblical Principles for Managing Your Money*
- *35 Keys to Financial Independence*
- *A Biblical Perspective On Tithing & Giving*
- *Basic Principles for Maximizing Your Personal Cash Flow*
- *Basic Principles of Conservative Investing*
- *Biblical Principles for Becoming Debt Free*
- *Biblical Principles for Building a Successful Business*
- *Biblical Principles for Financial Success – Student Workbook*
- *Biblical Principles for Financial Success – Teacher Workbook*
- *Biblical Principles for Personal Evangelism (out of print)*
- *Biblical Principles for Releasing Financial Provision*
- *Biblical Principles for Staying Out of Debt*
- *Biblical Principles for Success in Personal Finance*
- *Biblical Principles That Create Success Through Productivity*
- *Business, Occupations, Professions & Vocations in the Bible*
- *Family Finance Handbook*
- *Family Finance Student Workbook*
- *Family Finance Teacher Workbook*
- *Public Relations for the Local Church (out of print)*

Rich Brott and his wife, Karen, have been married for 35 years. He resides in Portland, Oregon, with his wife, three children, son-in-law and granddaughter.

Dedication

This book is dedicated to my 3 children: Julie, Jana and Nathaniel. They have brought nothing but joy to my life. It is my desire that they always follow the ways of God throughout their life. If they follow the biblical principles found in this book, I have no doubt that they will become successful in all that they choose to do.

Table of Contents

Introduction

While the Bible is full of principles to assist you in managing your money, just a few are mentioned in this book. Of course partnering with God in every area is basic, seeking His will and way first, focusing on giving rather than getting and understanding the principle of open heavens.

Resisting the views of the world in handling our personal finances means we do not trust in riches, money or possessions. These things will pass. But we do trust in God as our sole provider and the controller of our life.

Millions of people today are on a quest to accumulate possessions and wealth. It is hard to be content with what we have when the world's entire system is geared toward making us unhappy with everything we have and wanting everything we don't have. From advertising to attitude, we face a discontented culture. How much money does it take to be content? Usually just a little bit more. Money cannot buy contentment or happiness. It is hard for us to be satisfied with what we do have, but we need to strive for contentment and contend for happiness.

30 Biblical Principles for Managing Your Money also touches on the very practical issues of life and the very fundamental financial decisions that must be made. When you have debt, change is necessary. You must make a decision to change your attitude, lifestyle, spending habits and invest in a new you. Proverbs 22:7 says, "The rich rule over the poor, and the borrower is servant to the lender."

To Successful Money Management!
Rich Brott

Principle 1

The Biblical Principle of Knowing That God Owns It All

Psalm 50:10

"For every animal of the forest is mine, and the cattle on a thousand hills."

1 Chronicles 29:10-12

"'Praise be to you, O Lord, God of our father Israel, from everlasting to everlasting. Yours, O Lord, is the greatness and the power and the glory and the majesty and the splendor, for everything in heaven and earth is yours. Yours, O Lord, is the kingdom; you are exalted as head over all. Wealth and honor come from you; you are the ruler of all things. In your hands are strength and power.'"

Don't make the mistake of thinking your job or your business is what provides your income. God is the source of your abundant supply. Jobs disappear; customers in your business come and go. It is God who sees to it that your needs are being met. Everyone and everything else is just His instrument for getting it accomplished. God uses many vehicles to get the job done, but in the end, it is not us, but God's blessing upon our lives.

Haggai 2:8

"The silver is mine and the gold is mine, declares the Lord Almighty."

Billy Graham said, "If a person gets his attitude towards money straight, it will help straighten out almost every other area of his life. Tell me what you think about money, and I can tell you what you think about God, for these two are closely related. A man's heart is closer to his wallet than almost anything else."

Jesus taught that we must be responsible in our finances. God is the source of all wealth. He is the original owner of all things, for He made all things. As Scripture says, He owns the cattle on a thousand hills. In addition to the ways God provides for us supernaturally, God also gives us the ability to earn a living (see Deuteronomy 8:18).

When you partner with God in business, He not only will bless it, but He also will let you enjoy prosperity. But there is a caution not to keep everything to yourself. Instead of trying to figure out how little you can give to God, try giving it all to Him and ask Him how much you should keep. When you partner with God, He will prosper you! When God becomes your source, then your well will never run dry. When we become Christians, we become children of God, and the Bible says God wants to give gifts to His children.

A successful businessperson by the name of R. G. LeTourneau was in the business of manufacturing earth-moving equipment. As his business grew and prospered, he decided to increase his tithe over and above the tenth. In time, he eventually increased his giving to 90% of his income and lived on the rest. *Instead of giving the tenth, he lived the tenth.*

God blessed this man bountifully and used his inventive God-given genius and creativity to reach the world with the gospel. The Bible provides many great giving scriptures, but none seem more specific than that of the directive that every person should give what is in his heart, not reluctantly or under compulsion. Mr. LeTourneau certainly recognized the value of 2 Corinthians 9:7, and acknowledged that it was God who gave him the power to gain wealth.

Someone once said that the real measure of your wealth is how much you'd be worth if you lost all your money.

In the sixteenth century, Izaak Walton said, "Look to your health; and if you have it, praise God and value it next to conscience; for health is the second blessing that we mortals are capable of, a blessing money can't buy."

What does God already own that you are trying to keep absolute control over by refusing to acknowledge God's ownership? What about your business or your house? What about your transportation vehicles, your recreational vehicles, your clothes, toys and other worldly goods?

What about your body? According to Romans 12:1, your body belongs to the LORD. Does your time belong to you or to God? What about your income, your savings, your investments and your other possessions? Do these things belong to your or to God?

Have you been allowed oversight of them for the purpose of showing good stewardship or have you taken them over, assuming they are yours only? Everything you say, every decision you make, every action you take must be accountable to the principles of God.

What about your entire life? Your dreams, your goals, your visions; are they born of God or have you allowed your carnal nature to take complete control? Are you a thief or a steward? If a steward, then what kind of steward are you? Are you one that God can trust with complete care or are you careless in your stewardship?

Not only is the silver and the gold the LORD's, so is everything else. Everything belongs to God. So why not give it all to Him? In 1 Corinthians 4:2, Paul says it is required that those who have been given a trust must prove faithful. In other words, we are all stewards and must be the kind of stewards that are faithful. A steward is simply a manager of someone else's money and possessions. We must acknowledge God's ownership and manage it or use it as He would have us use it. We gain by giving; we lose by withholding.

Begin now to live a principled life.

Determine at this moment to live the principle of knowing that God owns it all!

Principle 2

The Biblical Principle of Seeking First

The biblical principle of seeking first is all about proper perspective and proper motives. If your sole purpose in life is to make money and accumulate *stuff* for yourself, then you are already headed down the wrong path.

Jesus said the kingdom of God is to be sought first. This does not mean to seek first for a while and then to switch to a second goal of accumulating vast amounts of material possessions second. It just means that our focus must always be on kingdom matters and kingdom priorities. As we keep our priorities in line, the things we need will be provided.

Jesus knew that men and women would have trouble keeping their hearts focused on their real purpose for being here. That's why, on the Sermon on the Mount, He said:

Matthew 6:19-21

> *"'Do not store up for yourselves treasures on earth, where moth and rust destroy, and where thieves break in and steal. But store up for yourselves treasures in heaven, where moth and rust do not destroy, and where thieves do not break in and steal. For where your treasure is, there your heart will be also.'"*

Matthew 6:33

> *" But seek first his kingdom and his righteousness, and all these things will be given to you as well."*

Putting God first in our lives alleviates us from the task of having to worry about everything else. Seeking His kingdom and righteousness first is simply making God the priority in our lives. Verse 33 outlines for us a priority, a principle and a promise. Our priority is to seek God's will and way first.

The principle is to focus on kingdom activity. The promise is that when we seek Him first and focus on the business of the kingdom, God will take care of all our other needs.

There is always the temptation to put our money first. Do you remember the rich young ruler who came to Jesus and said he wanted to follow Christ? How Jesus responded to Him didn't make him very happy. Jesus told him to give his money away and follow Him. You see, it wasn't the money that was wrong, it was that this young man placed his money ahead of and above all else.

"When wealth is lost, nothing is lost; when health is lost, something is lost; when character is lost, all is lost." – Billy Graham

If we have too much money, there is always the danger that we can depend upon it ultimately. Does your life reveal your desire to put God first? The Lord admonishes us to seek first His kingdom, His way of doing things, and not to worry about possessions. Acquisition of possessions never satisfies. We only want more and more. That is why our focus must be on needs, not wants.

What do we need? Generally that would include food and water, sunshine and air, rain and shelter. Beyond these basic survival needs could come the need for friends, family, relationships, self-esteem, etc. What we don't need is more things.

Materialism is a focus on things of matter rather than on the things of God. Before we put all our time, energy, interests and life into what we deem valuable, Jesus is telling us to stop and get your focus on things of eternal value.

Moses considered the reproach of Christ as greater riches than all the treasures in Egypt.

Hebrews 11:26

> *"He regarded disgrace for the sake of Christ as of greater value than the treasures of Egypt, because he was looking ahead to his reward."*

The biblical mandate is to seek first the things of the kingdom. The lives of believers are spoiled if they are completely wrapped up in possessions and absorbed in the pursuit of material accumulation.

We must ask God to help us develop an attitude of serving Him faithfully and a life that is free of debt so we can pursue the extension of kingdom priorities instead of human wants. After all, our whole purpose in life is to give to others, share with others and bless others just as we have been blessed.

Begin now to live a principled life. Determine at this moment to live the principle of seeking first!

Principle 3

The Biblical Principle of Giving, Not Getting

2 Corinthians 8:7

> *"But just as you excel in everything – in faith, in speech, in knowledge, in complete earnestness and in your love for us – see that you also excel in this grace of giving."*

Wealth

Is having a lot of money the key to everything? Does money bring happiness? Does money bring solutions to life's problems? If you had a limitless amount of money and could buy anything you wanted, what would you buy? When would you stop buying, gathering, grasping and grabbing? Our wealth does not come from what we accumulate in life, but from what we give in life.

Some of the wealthiest men in the world gathered in 1923 at the Edgewater Beach Hotel in Chicago. This group of seven was worth more than the entire U.S. Treasury in their time. These were great financial men with records of success who had achieved great prosperity.

But this was not the end of their story. Within 25 years the president of the largest steel company had died penniless. A millionaire wheat speculator had also become poor. Another, who was the president of the New York Stock Exchange, had already spent many years in prison.

Yet another of the wealthy seven who was a member of the president's cabinet had spent time in prison, but was pardoned so he could die at home instead of prison. The fifth of the seven committed suicide; the sixth man, who headed one of the world's largest companies, also took his own life. The seventh, and last of the world's richest men, also took his own life.

Acts 20:35

> *"Remembering the words the LORD Jesus himself said: 'It is more blessed to give than to receive.'"*

Luke 6:38

> *"Give, and it will be given to you. A good measure, pressed down, shaken together and running over, will be poured into your lap. For with the measure you use, it will be measured to you."*

"When it comes to giving until it hurts, most people have a very low threshold of pain." – Anonymous

Mother Teresa was a woman of God who never stopped giving of herself. She said, "Never worry about numbers. Help one person at a time, and always start with the person nearest you."

Grace

True givers are not motivated by competition; they are motivated by grace. What is this grace? In 2 Corinthians 8 and 9, it is referred to as a divine favor that is displayed in generosity. It is the divine enablement to participate greatly in giving. An act of grace as used in this passage means an act of giving.

Grace causes pleasure and is delightful; it means to be regarded favorably; it is a mercy that causes joy. Grace is that which makes one ready, quick, willing and prompt to give freely. Grace dignifies and lifts people up in its gift of favor; it honors and blesses and supplies all that is needed. Grace is the initiator of giving.

Neither biblical law, a set of rules, nor guilt or competition should make you give. It is grace that creates the desire to give, grace that gives us the ability to give and grace that causes us to move into the realm of faith. 2 Corinthians 8:6,7 says that giving is something we need to excel and abound in, but it must be motivated by grace.

"Never measure generosity by what you give, but by what you have left." – Fulton Sheen

Cheerful Giving

1 Chronicles 29:9

> *"Then the people rejoiced, for they had offered willingly, because with a loyal heart they had offered willingly to the Lord; and King David also rejoiced greatly" (NKJV).*

Giving should never be burdensome. It should never be stressful. Our gifts should not be presented in doubt, clothed in reluctance or reservation. In fact, giving, as seen in this passage, should be an occasion for great joy!

Our gifts should be presented in faith, presenting them to God with confidence in His Word. If we give with a grudging spirit and attitude, does it hinder God from giving us full blessing? I don't know. But what I do know is that God just simply loves one who gives cheerfully and wholeheartedly.

2 Corinthians 9:7

> *"Each man should give what he has decided in his heart to give, not reluctantly or under compulsion, for God loves a cheerful giver."*

In this verse it is clear that giving (we are not talking about returning God's tenth to Him) should not be coerced. No one should be intimidated into giving. No one should be pressured into giving. Giving must not be compulsory or motivated by guilt; it is to be exercised out of one's free will and love.

Giving is a personal decision to bless others as God has blessed us. We do this through supporting the various ministries of our local church. Yes, there are other giving opportunities, but be careful to first sustain the place where you are fed week in and week out. Take care to give willingly and cheerfully.

How should I give to the work of God?

Many churches offer opportunities to give to the Lord in a variety of ways. Check with your church for an avenue to give:

1. To the poor.
2. To the needs of children.
3. Toward retiring any debt the church has.
4. Toward new churches being planted.
5. Toward strategic, creative evangelism.
6. Toward constructing new buildings to be used for the purposes of God.
7. Toward Christian education (schools and colleges).
8. Toward the needs of the community (pregnancy centers, counseling, child abuse centers).

9. Toward the purchase of necessary equipment for your church.
10. Toward capital improvements for the church.
11. In the inheritance you will leave behind.

John Wesley donated to mission causes by sacrificing personal comforts. Living simply, he was able to give more than $500,000 to missions in his lifetime. When asked about this personal sacrifice, his answer was, "Gladly would I again make the floor my bed, a box my chair, a box my table, rather than that men should perish for want of the knowledge of the Savior."

During the World War II, Winston Churchill, then prime minister of Great Britain, set out to "win with words" over Hitler by raising the morale of the nation. Not only did he visit the troops and factories, but he also went to the out-of-the-way coal-mining towns. On one visit to the hard-working coal miners, the prime minister urged them to see their significance in the total effort for victory. He told them:

"We will be victorious! We will preserve our freedom. And years from now when our freedom is secure and peace reigns, your children and children's children will come and they will say to you, 'What did you do to win our freedom in that great war?' And one will say, 'I marched with the Eighth Army!' Someone else will proudly say, 'I manned a submarine.' And another will say, 'I guided the ships that moved the troops and supplies.' And still another will say, 'I doctored the wounds!'"

Then the great statesman paused. The dirty-faced miners sat in silence and awe, waiting for him to proceed.

"They will come to you," he shouted, "and you will say, with equal right and equal pride, 'I cut the coal! I cut the coal that fueled the ships that moved the supplies! That's what I did. I cut the coal!'"

We can all do our part. Maybe we are not on the frontlines, just like the coal miners in this story. However we can supply the fuel for these efforts. Our part is just as necessary as that person overseas; so let us partner together to fund God's kingdom.

Begin now to live a principled life. Determine at this moment to live the principle of giving, not getting!

Principle 4

The Biblical Principle of Supernatural Provision

1 Kings 17:15, 16

> *"So she went away and did according to the word of Elijah; and she and he and her household ate for many days. The bin of flour was not used up, nor did the jar of oil run dry, according to the word of the LORD which He spoke by Elijah" (NKJV).*

Supernatural provision happens when the natural is not enough. If we can make it happen on our own, there is no need for faith. No need for trusting God. And it follows that if we do not have faith and have no need for God, He will not step into areas we have reserved for our own self-control. The principle of supernatural provision is that He is strong when flesh cannot be.

Philippians 4:19

> *"And my God will meet all your needs according to his glorious riches in Christ Jesus."*

Notice that the scripture does not say, the company that employs you will provide for your needs. Neither does it say the local banker or loan officer will supply your needs. Nor does it say that the welfare department of your government will supply your needs. It says that God, and no one else, will supply your needs. God is your only Source! It's not your job that provides your income. It is God who provides your needs.

This story has been told for many generations. It is about a Christian family that was going through some tough times. They were so destitute that they didn't even have food for their next meal. The father and mother got down on their knees and cried out to God for food so their children would not go hungry.

A man who was not a Christian was walking by their house and heard their prayer. Instead of feeling bad for them, he decided to play a trick on them.

He went down to the grocery store and bought a huge box of groceries, put it on their front porch and rang the doorbell. When the Christian parents saw the groceries on the porch, they immediately began to thank God for it.

Just then the unbeliever walked up and said, "Why are you thanking God? I'm the one who placed the groceries there." The Christian father replied, "Oh no, it was God who answered our prayer and provided the groceries. But I do want to thank you for being His delivery boy and bringing them to us!"

God is your sole source, your only provider. Through Him and Him alone are all your needs met. Your professional employment is just that, it's not an end-all. When the economy tanks, so do jobs. When the industry sector that employs you goes bust, your job disappears with it. Don't trust your education, don't trust your experience, don't trust your job; trust God.

Begin now to live a principled life. Determine at this moment to live the principle of supernatural provision!

Principle 5

The Biblical Principle of Open Heavens

Deuteronomy 28:12

> *"The Lord will open the heavens, the storehouse of his bounty, to send rain on your land in season and to bless all the work of your hands. You will lend to many nations but will borrow from none."*

One way God opens the windows of heaven is by keeping us from untold financial disasters.

Malachi 3:10-11 says, "Bring ye all the tithes into the storehouse, that there may be meat in mine house, and prove me now herewith, saith the Lord of hosts, if I will not open you the windows of heaven, and pour you out a blessing, that there shall not be room enough to receive it. And I will rebuke the devourer for your sakes, and he shall not destroy the fruits of your ground; neither shall your vine cast her fruit before the time in the field, saith the Lord of hosts" (KJV).

What does it mean to "rebuke the devourer"? Many things create havoc in our financial lives. It may be the loss of a job, auto repair expenses, house maintenance, appliance breakdown, or healthcare related expenses. From time to time we all can acknowledge some difficulty in these areas. And when "out of nowhere" expenses come alongside us, they can be burdensome and costly.

However, what we don't know is all that God keeps away from us. When we are faithful in our giving, the Word simply states that our crops will be large and that He will keep the insects and plagues away. Whether you are a farmer, a tiller of the ground, or simply planting crops of a nonagricultural nature, you can rest assured God is working on your behalf.

Yet another way God opens the windows of heaven is by blessing us when we give. Generosity is God's antidote to greed. The heart and attitude of a blessed person is worth looking at. After all, do we not all want to be a blessed person? Blessed people are set apart in many ways because they have learned how to be blessed. We all have the opportunity to receive the blessing of God and be "under the shadow of the Almighty" (Psalm 91:1) if we so desire. The blessed person gives of his / her resources freely, cheerfully, and out of genuine appreciation to God.

When we look upon the attitudes and heart of a blessed person, what will we discover? What is the heart like? What kind of attitude does one need to receive the blessing? What about the heart of a blessed person?

What theme was so important to Jesus that He talked about it more than anything else? Was it heaven? Was it repentance? Was it prayer? Was it salvation? No. It was the subject of money. He knew that if He had our money, He would certainly have our hearts.

What about the attitude of a blessed person? Overall, the principal attitude must be that all money and all possessions belong to God. He trusts us with the care of these things until we prove ourselves unworthy of His trust. It is not our money, so it's not our problem to worry about it. It is our basic responsibility as good stewards to use it correctly.

Begin now to live a principled life. Determine at this moment to live the principle of open heavens!

Principle 6

The Biblical Principle of Kingdom Investing

Matthew 6:19-21

> *"Do not store up for yourselves treasures on earth, where moth and rust destroy, and where thieves break in and steal. But store up for yourselves treasures in heaven, where moth and rust do not destroy, and where thieves do not break in and steal. For where your treasure is, there your heart will be also."*

Most of us understand what we classify as earthly treasures. This list includes earthly possessions such as cars, boats, clothes, houses, bank accounts, jewelry, portfolios, etc.

In Scripture, Jesus is warning us about protecting our hearts from the love of these things, all of which can seem so real, so lasting, so concrete, but in reality can disappear so quickly. They can literally be here today, and gone tomorrow.

Death is the great equalizer, the constant leveler. Some of the ancient tombs discovered in the Middle East have been found packed with food and furniture, as well as slaves. Yet all of those buried remains, buried under sand for thousands of years, have done nothing for the one who spent a lifetime accumulating them.

Our stock portfolios are always in great risk to the ups and downs of the market, the wars and rumors of wars, the economy of the nation and world, and the integrity of the company management in which we invest. Our bodies and our minds, which may seem so healthy and sharp, may be wasted by disease or crushed by a mishap tomorrow.

We invest in what we care about. If we invest our money with God, we will be interested in the ministry advance of our local church and will pray for the expansion of His kingdom locally and globally.

Note, in the Matthew 6 passage, Jesus is not saying to have nothing, enjoy nothing or that possessions are a sin. Christ is saying to us to not get too tied to these things. Be a conduit, not a dam. *It is not about what we have, but what has us*. If you center your life on things, if you base your living upon possessions, you will for sure be disappointed.

Don't base your life, your future, your well being or your happiness on the things you have accumulated. Instead, be sure you lay up for yourself the real treasures, the ones that will be of eternal value.

Notice the tone of this Scripture (Matthew 6:19-21). It doesn't seem to be a suggestion, rather a definite command of sorts. It is no secret that the rich attract a lot of interested people. While he has money, everyone wants to be near him.

Should his riches disappear, so will his friends. Not much different from a beautiful, talented, young actress, singer or musician. When her beauty fades, or talent diminishes, the world looks for another to admire.

Many of the homes constructed in the ancient Middle East were made with sun-baked clay or loose stones. Although adequate for housing, it presented a comparatively easy way for thieves to dig under the wall, through the wall or by other means. No possessions were safe from those that would steal.

Of course, we know that rust can destroy even the best of tools and moths also attack things we consume. Literally, rust in its destructive path will eat into and can destroy nearly everything. Rust will eventually corrode all metal, including silver and gold. Figuratively speaking, rust can be anything that destroys you and your life. In short, all your treasures, whether physical or otherwise, can be destroyed.

The possessions we accumulate in this world are temporary at best. Each of the three metaphors found in Matthew 6:19-21 tell us together that life is short and futile. Anyone of these things, when expanded to include those things that can destroy from today's culture, clearly demonstrate to us the folly of putting our trust in earthly possessions. Bad investments, or good investments pilfered away by bad management or dishonest CEO's, can make our lifetime of savings disappear overnight.

It's not that saving or storing assets are in themselves sinful. Paul notes in 2 Corinthians 12:14 that parents ought to save up for their children. When increase comes our way, we should use it, not only for our needs, but also for the good of others.

Treasures on earth can become paths to building heavenly treasures if they are used and distributed for the Glory of God. Jesus understood clearly that in the consumer culture of this world, a constant battleground for our affections, our hearts and our souls rage.

"Our callings are not simply secular means of making money or a living, but are God's means of utilizing our gifts and interests to His glory." – a paraphrase of Martin Luther (1483 – 1546)

"Alas, how many, even among those who are called believers, have plenty of all the necessities of life, and yet complain of poverty!" – John Wesley (1703 – 1791)

"Money never made a man happy yet, nor will it. There is nothing in its nature to produce happiness. The more a man has, the more he wants. Instead of its filling a vacuum, it makes one. If it satisfies one want, it doubles and trebles that want another way. That was a true proverb of the wise man, rely upon it; 'Better is little with the fear of the Lord, than great treasure, and trouble therewith.'" – Benjamin Franklin (1706 – 1790)

Begin now to live a principled life. Determine at this moment to live out the principle of kingdom investing!

Principle 7

The Biblical Principle of First Things First

Personal prosperity will never come at the expense of ethical values and biblical principles. Settle it once and for all in your heart and mind. God values obedience and makes it a condition of His blessing.

Until your personal life and financial life get in line with His morality and commandments, don't expect financial miracles to be the norm in your life. Those who have not learned this lesson often struggle for years with the burden of heavy debt.

An interesting group of Scriptures surround the story of rebuilding the ancient Temple. The main characters in this story are Joshua the high priest, Zerubbabel the governor of Judah, Haggai the prophet and the Israelites.

It seems they had become so involved in their own personal lives and building their own houses, that they had neglected the building, finishing and operational needs of God's house.

God apparently finally had His fill of the people's inability to focus upon the principle of "first things first," and He sent word to the governor through Haggai the prophet. The message to be delivered was straightforward, direct, to the point and quite harsh. He stated their current condition, summarized the problem and stated the result. There is nothing ambiguous about the mind of God.

Haggai 1:5-10

> *"Look at the result: You plant much but harvest little. You have scarcely enough to eat or drink and not enough clothes to keep you warm. Your income disappears, as though you*

> *were putting it into pockets filled with holes! 'Think it over,' says the* L*ORD* *Almighty. 'Consider how you have acted and what has happened as a result! Then go up into the mountains, bring down timber, and rebuild my Temple, and I will be pleased with it and appear there in my glory,' says the* L*ORD*. *'You hope for much but get so little. And when you bring it home, I blow it away – it doesn't last at all. Why? Because my Temple lies in ruins, and you don't care. Your only concern is your own fine homes. That is why I am holding back the rains from heaven and giving you such scant crops'" (TLB).*

What are you doing in your personal financial life that is not pleasing to God? Why are you out of the flow of God's divine blessing? How many problems have you brought into your life because you have failed to line up with the principles of God's Word?

Don't you think it is time for you to assess your current lifestyle and make the proper adjustments needed to bring your life back in line? It is never too late to begin again. God is awesome and full of mercy. But He does want your priorities to be in line with the Word. Get your financial priorities straight and watch the blessings of heaven begin to flow in your direction.

Begin now to live a principled life. Determine at this moment to live out the principle of first things first!

Principle 8

The Biblical Principle of Being Proactive

Matthew 17:27

> *"Go to the lake and throw out your line. Take the first fish you catch; open its mouth."*

Nothing will be thrown into our laps. No, financial prosperity is not an unconditional providential blessing, and yes, conditions are attached. We are to take action and be proactive.

The abilities and giftings God provides motivate us to action. Sometimes it takes our persistence in doing the same things faithfully with the heart of a servant. Other times, it is time to try new things, new methods and seek new opportunities. Sometimes the steady plodding brings the success of the blessed life.

God allows us to possess certain things, but mere possession is not ownership. Those things you possess can be taken from you in an instant. The scores of dishonest accounting firms and corrupt corporate CEO's of our day have seen to that. Billions of honest dollars invested by millions of wage earners have disappeared. Wage earners have seen their retirement savings disappear in a matter of mere months.

You can possess, but it is God who owns. You may earn a living, but it is God who gives to you the ability to earn. God is the one who gives to you the power to get wealth.

Let's note what Scriptures say about just how much you really own.

Deuteronomy 8:18

"But remember the LORD your God, for it is he who gives you the ability to produce wealth".

Psalm 24:1

"The earth is the LORD's, and everything in it, the world, and all who live in it."

Psalm 50:10, 11

"For every animal of the forest is mine, and the cattle on a thousand hills. I know every bird in the mountains, and the creatures of the field are mine."

Psalm 100:3

"Know that the LORD is God. It is he who made us, and we are his; we are his people, the sheep of his pasture."

Ezekiel 18:4

"For every living soul belongs to me."

Haggai 2:8

"'The silver is mine and the gold is mine,' declares the LORD Almighty."

Acts 17:28

"For in him we live and move and have our being."

Romans 12:1

"Therefore, I urge you, brothers, in view of God's mercy, to offer your bodies as living sacrifices, holy and pleasing to God."

Ecclesiastes 9:11

> *"The race is not to the swift or the battle to the strong, nor does food come to the wise or wealth to the brilliant or favor to the learned; but time and chance happen to them all."*

Hebrews 12:1, 2
This verse tells us what to do and what to avoid:

> *"Let us throw off everything that hinders and the sin that so easily entangles, and let us run with perseverance the race marked out for us. Let us fix our eyes on Jesus, the author and perfecter of our faith."*

Being a person of principle requires hard work, diligence and proactivity. Nothing will be handed to you without these requirements. The Bible says that if a person does not work, he should not eat. Now that's a pretty simple yet direct statement. Does God want to bless us supernaturally? Of course, He does. Will His blessing come to us if we are lazy, idle, slothful, passive and unwilling to roll up our sleeves and get to work? No, I don't believe so.

Proverbs 21:5

> *"Steady plodding brings prosperity; hasty speculation brings poverty" (TLB).*

Proverbs 21:25, 26

> *"The sluggard's craving will be the death of him, because his hands refuse to work. All day long he craves for more, but the righteous give without sparing."*

Taking action, being proactive, not giving up – all are principles for living the life of a blessed person.

Begin now to live a principled life. Determine at this moment to live the principle of being proactive!

Principle 9

The Biblical Principle of Resisting Worldviews

Resisting the views of the world in handling our personal finances means we don't trust in riches, money or possessions. These things will surely pass away. But we do trust in God. He is our sole provider and should be in control of our lives.

We live in a culture that continuously encourages us to buy, buy, buy. From billboards to television commercials, from radio advertisements to magazine ads, we are told about everything we don't have, but must have right away. It takes a lot of stamina just to resist accepting what society tries to impose upon our thinking. The Bible cautions us in these matters and encourages us to withstand such pressure.

Romans 12:2

> *"Don't copy the behavior and customs of this world, but be a new and different person with a fresh newness in all you do and think. Then you will learn from your own experience how his ways will really satisfy you" (TLB).*

Our culture and society have sold us a bill of goods. They teach us that to be happy we have to have certain things. We must refuse to accept the world's view of wealth, happiness and possessions.

We do not have to have it all! We don't have to wear just the right clothes, drive that certain brand of car, have the latest model available, buy a bigger home, own six televisions, possess the latest digital camera, and carry a dozen credit cards in our wallets to be fulfilled.

We must not allow the world to dictate its view of what possessions we should own. The world should not be allowed to design our lifestyle. The world should not tell us what success is and what the picture of affluence should look like. Success is doing what God desires.

Success and wealth look different from a Christian perspective. Wealth is having what you need. Wealth is more than money. It is having a local church that inspires you to draw close to God. It is having a loving spouse and the blessing of children. Wealth is enjoying great health and great relationships. Wealth is having good friends.

The world's view in our society is to look for ways to make a lot of money, very quickly, by doing little work. A constant lookout for get-rich schemes is prevalent.

The biblical principle centers on productivity, hard work, personal diligence and God's blessing. We are to use our God-given talents to partner with God's wisdom. If God chooses to bless us with wealth, then we properly use the riches God allows us to extend and further His kingdom.

Reject the world-view of materialism and self-centeredness at any cost. You won't benefit from having it all. If you have a family, trying to have it all will be a detriment to spiritual growth and may even cause major missteps in later years.

Pray when tempted to jump at the latest scheme. If you have trouble resisting the constant bombardment of advertisements that make you want to go out and make an immediate purchase, shut off the television or turn down the radio.

There is another way: be a good steward of God's gifts to you. Be careful what you do with your money, for someday you will have to account for how you used God's blessing. Every purchase you make should be a spiritual decision. After all, you are using His resources.

Begin now to live a principled life. Determine at this moment to live the principle of resisting worldviews!

Principle 10

The Biblical Principle of Temporary Possessions

1 Timothy 6:7, 8

> *"For we brought nothing into the world, and we can take nothing out of it."*

You will do well to remember that money and possessions are, at best, temporary. At most, money only lasts a lifetime. At worst, it doesn't last at all. It is very fleeting, only a vapor, just like our lives.

Psalm 39:4

> *"Show me, O Lord, my life's end and the number of my days; let me know how fleeting is my life."*

Don't spend all your life trying to accumulate something that will never last. How much better it would be to spend your time investing in things of eternal nature. Being the recipient of God's provision and blessing and enjoying great wealth and prosperity is not meant for the purpose of accumulating earthly temporary gain.

It is to be used to build a foundation for heavenly gain. Instead of hoarding it all for personal enjoyment, it is to be used to further the kingdom of God. Any prosperity you gain on this earth is because you have learned good stewardship principles. The biblical prosperity here in this life is but a foreshadow of things to come on the other side.

At the end of your life, will you look back and wish you would have owned a bigger home or a nicer car, or that you had spent more time with your family and friends? The only thing you can (and will) take out of this life is your soul. How much time do you spend daily pursuing eternal possessions instead of temporal ones?

On judgment day, will God be able to say to you, "Well done my good and faithful servant"? Will He be pleased with the way you spent your days here on earth or will He be saddened by the amount of time you wasted on accumulating material possessions instead of eternal ones?

Possessions are temporary! Don't make the mistake of holding on to them too tightly. Job understood this when he said in chapter one, verse twenty, "Naked I came from my mother's womb, and naked I will depart. The Lord gave and the Lord has taken away; may the name of the Lord be praised."

It may be pleasant to accumulate many comforts of living, but just be sure you understand their temporary value and nature. To spend a lifetime gathering temporary possessions but neglecting the important treasures that last an eternity would be very foolish indeed.

Don't get so focused on the here and now and in things of temporary value that you fail to think and see eternally. Treasure those things that have eternal and kingdom value. The only treasure worth possessing is kingdom or eternal treasure.

Matthew 6:19-21

> *"Do not store up for yourselves treasures on earth, where moth and rust destroy, and where thieves break in and steal. But store up for yourselves treasures in heaven, where moth and rust do not destroy, and where thieves do not break in and steal. For where your treasure is, there your heart will be also."*

Psalm 89:47

> *"Remember how fleeting is my life. For what futility you have created all men!"*

Proverbs 21:6

> *"A fortune made by a lying tongue is a fleeting vapor and a deadly snare."*

Begin now to live a principled life. Determine at this moment to live the principle of temporary possessions!

Principle 11

The Biblical Principle of Contentment

1 Timothy 6:8

> *"But if we have food and clothing, we will be content with that."*

Millions of people today are on a quest to accumulate possessions and wealth. It is hard to be content with what we have when the world's entire system is geared toward making us unhappy with everything we have and wanting everything we don't have.

From advertising to attitude, we face a discontented culture. How much money does it take to be content? Usually just a little bit more. Money cannot buy contentment or happiness. It is hard for us to be satisfied with what we do have, but we need to strive for contentment and contend for happiness.

"Contentment is a pearl of great price, and whoever procures it at the expense of ten thousand desires makes a wise and a happy purchase." - John Balguy

Making money is certainly not wrong, as long as it does not violate the laws of our land and the principles of God's Word. The all-for-me and none-for-others way of man's thinking is immoral. People of principle who subscribe to the values of the Bible will be good stewards if they obey the law of giving. They will find happiness in exact proportion to the degree in which they give. They will be content with life and all that it affords.

Money and happiness are not mutually exclusive. Benjamin Franklin noted, "Money never made a man happy yet, nor will it. There is nothing in its nature to produce happiness. The more a man has, the more he wants. Instead of filling a vacuum, it makes one." He also said, "Contentment makes poor men rich; discontentment makes rich men poor."

Being a good steward begins with the blessing of God, but the test and fruit of good stewardship is how we use those blessings. Are we a conduit or do we stop the stream of God's favor. Do we allow the river to flow, or do we dam up God's supply? To me it is a matter of management, not ownership. Are we to give only a little and hoard the rest for our own pleasure? I think not.

God expects us to use what we need (He has promised to supply our need), then to multiply and return the rest. Stewardship is trust, knowing and disbursing His blessing. The blessing of stewardship is in giving.

Many wealthy people wish they had friends. Some of the most prominent people in the world are some of the saddest people on earth. Even their money cannot hide their unhappiness and displeasure with life. It is sad when people spend an entire lifetime trying to get rich, only to find that when they finally become rich, they are still unhappy, still dissatisfied with life and still sad.

Jesus let us know in Luke 12:15 that a person's life and happiness do not consist of things, possessions and money. In other words, all the possessions in the world will not bring contentment, nor will they buy happiness.

When the rich man in Luke 12:19 declared that after working hard for many years, accumulating great wealth and all the goods his world could offer him, he could now be free to take it easy by eating, drinking and be merry. He had dedicated his whole life to accumulating great possessions for such a time as this.

Jesus called this man a fool because of his thinking. His thinking was wrong, his priorities were wrong and because of wrong thinking, he was unable to be the kind of good steward he was required to be.

The Christian is not to love money. He is to love God. The Scripture is not much concerned about our having wealth, but is concerned with how it is obtained and how it is managed. God allows us to be partners with Him. God's role in the partnership is to meet our needs (Philippians 4:19). Our role in the partnership is to work (2 Thessalonians. 3:10). Our work is a means of worship and ministry. When we work, we meet the needs of our family and serve the LORD at the same time. We are also to work with proper motives (Colossians 3:23,24).

The rich man, whom Jesus called a fool, was an example of a person who loved money more than life itself. But God had other plans for him. After calling the man a fool and after working selfishly for a lifetime just so he could retire in pleasure and ease, God said that tonight was his last evening on earth.

Harmful Desires

1 Timothy 6:9

"People who want to get rich fall into temptation and a trap and into many foolish and harmful desires that plunge men into ruin and destruction."

Not Loving Money

1 Timothy 6:10

"For the love of money is a root of all kinds of evil. Some people, eager for money, have wandered from the faith and pierced themselves with many griefs."

All About Greed

Luke 12:16-18

"The ground of a certain rich man produced a good crop. He thought to himself, What shall I do? I have no place to store my crops. Then he said, 'This is what I'll do. I will tear down my barns and build bigger ones, and there I will store all my grain and my goods.'"

In this passage Jesus is telling us that we should find contentment in what we have instead of living in the discontent of what we do not have. We are to be grateful for what we have been blessed with and stop always striving for more. "Now godliness with contentment is great gain" (I Timothy 6:6; NKJV).

Genesis 2:15, 16

"The Lord God placed the man in the Garden of Eden as its gardener, to tend and care for it. But the Lord God gave the man this warning: 'You may eat any fruit in the garden except fruit from the Tree of Conscience – for its fruit will open your eyes to make you aware of right and wrong, good and bad. If you eat its fruit, you will be doomed to die.'"

Genesis 3:1-6

"The serpent was the craftiest of all the creatures the Lord God had made. So the serpent came to the woman. 'Really?' he asked. 'None of the fruit in the garden? God says you mustn't eat any of it?' 'Of course we may eat it,' the woman told him. 'It's only the fruit from the tree at the center of the garden that we are not to eat. God says we mustn't eat

it or even touch it, or we will die.' 'That's a lie!' the serpent hissed. 'You'll not die! God knows very well that the instant you eat it you will become like him, for your eyes will be opened – you will be able to distinguish good from evil!' The woman was convinced. How lovely and fresh looking it was! And it would make her so wise! So she ate some of the fruit and gave some to her husband, and he ate it too."

Genesis 3:23

"So the LORD God banished him forever from the Garden of Eden, and sent him out to farm the ground from which he had been taken" (TLB).

Very little commentary is needed here. Adam and Eve had the privilege of living in a garden so beautiful, that it was nearly indescribable. They could enjoy its beauty and bask in its atmosphere and eat of its fruit, save one tree. Yet they were not content and sought to have everything, when they actually needed nothing else. The result was personally devastating to them.

Begin now to live a principled life. Determine at this moment to live the principle of contentment!

Principle 12

The Biblical Principle of Proper Motives

God is interested in your motives. Can you be trusted with prosperity? If you cannot be trusted now in poverty, why should you be given prosperity? Jesus said in Matthew 6:33, "But seek ye first the kingdom of God, and his righteousness; and all these things shall be added unto you" (KJV).

How much money, health, wealth, position, prominence and influence can God trust you to handle? Have you been 100% trustworthy in the past with all that God has given to you? If not, why should He give you more?

Do you give a full day's work to your employer for a fair wage in return? If not, why should he trust you with a better job? Are you a good steward with the wage he has given to you? Are you judicious about how you spend your earnings? If not, why should you be trusted with a higher rate of pay if you are not a good financial manager with what you have already been given?

Do you maintain your car, truck, home, etc. now? If you cannot be responsible now for taking care of the possessions God has already given you, why should He bless you with more?

If God were to look down upon you with the idea of blessing you beyond your expectations, but first checked your money motive, what would He find? Would you be the one He can trust with great wealth, knowing you would use it to bless the kingdom of God? Or would you be the one who would simply use it to gain more personal possessions and to live a life of personal fulfillment and easy living?

The focus of many people is pleasure, sensual indulgence, money, selfishness, power and flattery. People who live this way do nothing of lasting or eternal value. They have no ultimate purpose in mind. As Christians, we need to have eternal values and purpose in mind.

Our motives and priorities must be God and His kingdom first, me last. Sometimes we get jealous of the success of others who are not Christians. They seem to be happy and rich and enjoying a life of luxury. A musician and prophet in Old Testament times by the name of Asaph, said, "I was envious at the foolish, when I saw the prosperity of the wicked" (Psalm 73:3).

Ungodly men and women may achieve material prosperity apart from God, but they can never achieve the deep settled peace that comes from God. Riches gained without God are a snare and do not bring peace. Prosperity that comes from God brings not only an abundance of possessions, but also emotional peace, happiness and great joy.

Do you know why some wicked people are rich today? The Bible provides a simple explanation. The wicked who are rich are simply holding the wealth that someday God will give to His children.

> *"And the wealth of the sinner is laid up for the righteous" (Proverbs 13:22; ASV).*

In the Old Testament, Solomon tells us in Proverbs 22:7 that the borrower is a servant to the lender. In the New Testament a passage in Luke 16:13 says, "No servant can serve two masters. Either he will hate the one and love the other, or he will be devoted to the one and despise the other. You cannot serve both God and money."

Both Scripture passages confirm each other. How can you properly serve God when you are a slave or servant to a creditor. When you want to follow God wholeheartedly but are a slave to debt, a conflict of interest arises. You need to be debt free to follow the will of God for your life. While your creditors are not concerned about God's will for you, they do want their money returned to them.

Your heart concerning the kingdom of God may be proper and principled, but if your motives and decisions are influenced at all by a love for money or the things money can buy, your thinking is tarnished. If your thinking remains tainted, it won't be long until your heart is also corrupted.

Begin now to live a principled life. Determine at this moment to live the principle of proper motives!

Principle 13

The Biblical Principle of Financial Stewardship

Luke 16:11, 12

> *"So if you have not been trustworthy in handling worldly wealth, who will trust you with true riches? And if you have not been trustworthy with someone else's property, who will give you property of your own?"*

Every human being alive must be a steward of personal resources of skill, knowledge, strength, possessions and influence. We don't need to necessarily aspire for more or feel discouraged about areas of what we may perceive as lack, we just need to use what we have.

Hard work, efficient use of our available resources, and a disciplined personal life will lead to prosperity and success. Os Guinness said, "Ownership is God's; stewardship is ours."

Matthew 25:24-28

> *"Then the man with the $1,000 came and said, 'Sir, I knew you were a hard man, and I was afraid you would rob me of what I earned, so I hid your money in the earth and here it is!' But his master replied, 'Wicked man! Lazy slave! Since you knew I would demand your profit, you should at least have put my money into the bank so I could have some interest. Take the money from this man and give it to the man with the $10,000'" (TLB).*

In Matthew 25:14-30 the parable of the talents is recorded. This story tells of a certain man who distributed his wealth among three servants, giving to each according to his ability. As this parable would imply, our abilities vary individually, and it is wise for us to realize that this is true also in our ability to earn money.

The parable proceeds to tell how each man invested his seed money. The first two traded theirs, that is they used it, and in the process they doubled the amount they had originally. The last person, however, tried to hoard or keep his by doing nothing with it. In the end, each had to account for his actions.

The man with only two talents, through his small ability and industry, gained a 100% increase, and he was promoted. He was responsible only to use the ability he had to do the best he could do. What about the man who had one talent? According to the Bible, his complaining and whining attitude was not well received. His employer, though critical, was just in his actions. He told the slothful servant that he could have tried at the least to obtain help from others by placing the talent into the hands of those who knew what to do with it.

Instead, the man chose idleness. He was cast away and punished, not because he misused the talent or lost it or sold it, but because he did nothing with it.

God expects us to be doing what we are able to do with what He has committed to us. If we apply ourselves, and use the talents He has given us, He will bless us. If you are a good steward over a little, then God looks at you and thinks, I can trust this person with more.

Revelation 2:23

"I will repay each of you according to your deeds."

Begin now to live a principled life. Determine at this moment to live the principle of financial stewardship!

Principle 14

The Biblical Principle of Financial Supply

Matthew 17:26

> *"So go down to the shore and throw in a line, and open the mouth of the first fish you catch. You will find a coin to cover the taxes for both of us; take it and pay them" (TLB).*

One of the wonderful principles of the Bible is that of divine supply; God promises to supply our every need. Financial supply is a God-given gift.

God gives us many gifts, but His greatest gift was His death on the cross, providing a living sacrifice for our sins. He has given us the gift of salvation. He gives us the gift of life, of family, of friends and of good health. The Bible says that He loves to give us good gifts.

Matthew 7:11

> *"If you, then, though you are evil, know how to give good gifts to your children, how much more will your Father in heaven give good gifts to those who ask him!"*

If a gift is promised, but not yet given, why do some people borrow and go into debt just to obtain what God had intended to supply anyway? Is this because of our impatience or a lack of trust? Is it because we don't really have faith for God's abundant supply or don't agree with His timetable?

When two people marry in the traditional Christian wedding, the vow includes the statement, "until death do us part." Many good marriages break apart because of a great wall of debt. Unfortunately, in our current culture, this sacred vow might be more accurate had it said, "until debt do us part."

Many statistics now conclude that the majority of all divorces are influenced by financial controversy and seemingly insurmountable debt. Debt can be avoided in most cases. Most borrowing and getting into debt is not the result of unplanned medical expenses, but rather deliberate choices to burden oneself with more financial obligation.

If you know that most borrowing is not necessary and most debt can be avoided, and that your heavenly Father will provide for your needs, why then do you want to put your financial life in jeopardy by taking on more debt? You can be sure of these things:

- God knows your need.
- He wants to provide for you.
- He desires to bless you with good gifts.

Everything we have is a gift from the LORD. He desires to bless and prosper you. Jeremiah 29:11 says, "For I know the plans I have for you," declares the LORD, "plans to prosper you and not to harm you, plans to give you hope and a future."

Along with these gifts come personal responsibility. Jesus talked about stewardship a great deal. *Jesus dealt with money matters, because money matters!*

Both Jesus and Satan know that "where your treasure is, there your heart will be also" (Matthew 6:21). That's why both are very interested in what we do with our money.

Our attitude toward money is a spiritual matter! If our attitude is right, we will be good stewards of all God has allowed us to oversee, and by doing so, an unending supply of provision will come our way.

Begin now to live a principled life. Determine at this moment to live the principle of financial supply!

Principle 15

The Biblical Principle of Seeking Counsel

2 Chronicles 18:4

> *"But Jehoshaphat also said to the king of Israel, 'First seek the counsel of the Lord.'"*

Hosea 4:6

> *"My people are destroyed from lack of knowledge."*

Families are faced with many financial challenges and decision-making opportunities. It is a good thing we are not able to see into the future or we might become very discouraged indeed. But such is life! We take the good with the bad, and somehow it all seems to come out okay.

Financial decisions are a regular part of life. We cannot get around them, but we can learn to handle them effectively. Satisfactory solutions must be found to complicated questions. What to do about housing? Should one rent or buy? How to get out of debt? How to stay out of debt? Is certain debt bad? Can debt ever be considered good? Various resources can be used to solve these problems and to achieve individual family goals.

Other questions include: How can we keep ahead of the bills when the family is growing and needing so many things? Can we afford to finance a new car? How do we know if we are saving enough money? These are important questions and each raises a particular concern.

Be assured that not any one answer will suit all individuals and families.

The questions raised can be answered by tackling one challenge or problem at a time. Part of the answer is simply recognizing the problem and then solving it or answering each question one at a time. By doing so, people can be productive and cope with the difficult decisions better. An added plus is receiving the satisfaction that comes from being in control of your financial life.

Although the answers to these personal financial questions may differ from person to person, the method of arriving at the answers can be similar.

Each question answered, and each financial problem solved can move your family and you one step closer to your goals. If you find that your goals and objectives are not being met, then possibly not all of the problems have been completely solved.

Isaiah 30:1

> *"Woe to the rebellious children," says the Lord, "Who take counsel, but not of Me, and who devise plans, but not of My Spirit" (NKJV).*

Isaiah 16:3

> *"Give us counsel, render a decision."*

Let's look at some steps toward solving those financial challenges.

Seeking Improvement

Facing financial challenges begins with knowing that a situation can be better. The process starts by realizing the difference between what is and what ought to be, and then wanting to do something about it. If you don't know that a situation can be better, you will hardly be ready to solve a problem. You must be aware that challenges do, in fact exist, before they can be solved. Once the awareness is there, you can then seek the answer.

Clarifying Goals

Facing financial challenges means having a clear definition and understanding of individual and family financial goals. Sit down as a family and put on paper those personal goals that you wish to accomplish. Prioritize them, rating their importance.

If you have children, perhaps you want each of them to have some exposure to music; if so, then music lessons might be a family goal. But you may have other family goals that do not include music. By listing those goals, you can measure any success in terms of the goals that are achieved. A clear definition of those goals is necessary before you can begin your journey.

Defining the Problem

Facing financial challenges means that once the goals are known, the problem needs to be defined. After you identify your goal, you are ready to state the challenge or obstacle that stands in the way of reaching it. More than one obstacle may become apparent.

Possibly several solutions will have to be found. Financial challenges need to be defined carefully. If they are formulated only in vague and general terms, the solutions are apt to be vague and general, too. Problems can also be studied more easily if they are stated in relationship to your goals. Stating the problem helps keep the goal in focus and the problem in perspective.

As you attend to one goal, you'll find it related to other goals. In this way, an overall view is necessary; a snapshot is not enough. Seldom can a problem be considered individually. The solution to one puzzle may alter other solutions, or it may introduce new problems and obstacles. This process of problem solving goes on and on. It can never stop, and must be continual.

Determining Resources

Facing financial challenges means that after the challenge is stated, the available resources need to be determined. What resources are available or can be made available that might contribute to the solution of the challenge or problem? Resources are the tools that will help you reach your goals. Human resources will include your own personal skills, talents, knowledge, health and energy. Material resources include your money, house, household equipment (camera, mower, washer and dryer, sewing machine, computer), vehicles and so forth. Each of these things has potential to generate additional income to meet a specific family goal.

Outlining Alternatives

Facing financial challenges means that alternative solutions to the challenge need to be outlined. Once the…

a) financial challenge has been identified
b) the goals defined
c) resources evaluated

…then all the alternatives need to be outlined. This will provide an opportunity to select the most satisfying solution. This process may require additional information. After alternative solutions to a problem have been outlined, each choice must be evaluated in terms of its outcome.

The need for factual and instructive information becomes even greater when seeking solutions involving expensive purchases. In many cases special support may be needed, and assistance from experts may help. Until such information is obtained, an individual or family is not in a position to make those decisions or choose between solutions with confidence.

Making a Decision

Facing financial challenges means that after the alternatives have been analyzed, it is time to make a decision. The moment comes to decide on adopting one of the possible solutions. The decision must be made and acted upon, and the results evaluated.

Summary

Managing your finances involves financial problem solving by choosing among alternative solutions to each challenge. To start with, realize that a problem (such as managing your credit or getting out from under a heavy burden of debt) exists. In other words, something about the present practice or procedure isn't satisfactory, and must be changed.

If it seems nothing is being accomplished, then the current circumstances are probably not acceptable. To know what needs to be accomplished, the goals must be defined. The real purpose for solving the problems confronting us is to achieve particular goals.

In reaching those goals, we can state the challenge or problem that has become an obstacle. Then, after seeing more precisely the problem or challenge, we must determine what we have to work with by taking inventory of our resources.

Keeping our resources in mind, we are ready to outline the possible solutions to the problem (identify the alternatives) and how each solution is likely to work out. On the basis of our analysis of the possible outcomes, a decision can be made about a solution.

The decision must then be acted upon, that is, it must be implemented. After a period of time, the results can be evaluated through various means of measurement.

Begin now to live a principled life. Determine at this moment to live the principle of seeking counsel!

Principle 16

The Biblical Principle of Managing Possessions

Because we are not our own, we should dedicate to God all that we are, all that we own, and all that we will ever be. You are God's, so all you have belongs to God. You simply manage your possessions for Him. Your business belongs to God. When everything you have belongs to God, it takes off all of the pressure.

In many countries, citizens pride themselves in private property ownership. In reality, all property, possessions, money and wealth belong to God. We are simply managers of what belongs to Him. All the land and all property still belong to the Creator.

The Bible offers many stories and illustrations of approval of wealth. But according to Scripture, riches are a gift and a special blessing. Wealth was given by God on many occasions to meet the needs of the poor, not just for having more. It is clear that accumulating wealth is meant for kingdom purposes. The rich are to be good stewards of their resources, for they have come from God.

1 Corinthians 6:19, 20

> *"You are not your own; you were bought at a price. Therefore honor God with your body."*

When your possessions and business belong to God, you are not responsible for their ultimate success. Of course, you are required to be a good manager. Let's say you are a farmer and your farm belongs to God. If the weather is dry and it doesn't rain, you don't have to worry about it because it belongs to God. If your business is dedicated to God, it becomes His problem and not yours.

The apostle Paul realized that although everything in the universe belongs to God, if we team up with Him, He allows us to keep some of everything He provides.

Paul said that the soldiers in the army do not pay for their own expenses. The farmer who harvests the crop has a right to eat some of it. The one who plants the vineyard gets to enjoy some of its fruit.

Luke 1:52, 53

> *"He has brought down rulers from their thrones but has lifted up the humble. He has filled the hungry with good things but has sent the rich away empty."*

Luke 1:53 profiles some rich people of Jesus' day. The rich hoarded all their possessions and treasures. They did not share their resources with the poor and needy. They believed God approved of them and their lifestyle so He gave them great wealth.

Because of this erroneous attitude, they looked down upon the poor as being people that did not have the favor and blessing of God. They idolized their wealth and held it very close. Their very identity was defined in how much money they had and the possessions they gathered around them.

In Jesus' day, many common and ordinary people were very poor, but they were not poor because God did not love them. Nor were they poor because of their own personal failings or lack of intelligence. They were not lazy, they worked hard, yet were very poor.

Many could not even provide the essentials for themselves and their families. They were vulnerable to the rich and powerful of their time. They had no way to improve their economic condition or their family social status.

Today, many people find their own sense of worth and identity in what they have, where they can travel to and what kind of possessions they have accumulated. We need to be wise and watch that our own sense of value comes solely from our inner spiritual character and not from what we have or what we possess.

Our *stuff* should never have a firm grip on us – not on our attitude, not on our character, and not on our sense of self-worth. Our outward behavior should reflect our inner spirituality. Our actions should be an outgrowth of our character. We are not owners or possessors. We are but managers of the temporary allowances of God.

Begin now to live a principled life. Determine at this moment to live the principle of managing possessions!

Principle 17

The Biblical Principle of Appropriate Use

Is it wrong to have money? Does being spiritual mean you must give up all your possessions and live in poverty? Are possessions bad? Doesn't the Scripture say money is the root of all evil? Of course, the accurate and truthful answer to each of these questions is "no."

The Bible does say in I Timothy 6:10 that the "love" of money is the root of all evil. God created the world. God created all the varied pleasures of life itself. 1 Timothy 4 lets us know that everything God created was good, and that nothing is to be rejected when it is received with thanksgiving. Satan did not, and cannot, create anything. All he can do is attempt to corrupt every good thing God has given to us.

Mark 10 tells us the story of the rich young ruler. Here was a decent person, one who had worked hard and who had become very wealthy. We are not told that he had any real problems with theft, murder, adultery, perjury or anything else. In fact, he admits to living by the Ten Commandments from a very young age.

The rich young ruler wanted eternal or everlasting life. But when Jesus the Everlasting Life looked into his eyes and said to give all he had to the poor and follow Him, the cost seemed too high. Jesus did say, that by doing so, the young ruler would have treasure in heaven. But the young man went away sad.

What was the rich young ruler's situation? Was it that he had too much money and that people with great wealth cannot go to heaven? Of course not! His stumbling block was that his wealth had him. Possessions and money are not bad – in fact they are good when used as tools to support the kingdom of God.

The young man suffered from foolish decision making. When the greatest opportunity of his life was staring him in the face, he chose to reject it in favor of his money. He had not learned the principle of appropriate use.

It is not all about having great wealth and using it the wrong way. Many Christians have very little money, yet have to overcome the same obstacle as the rich young ruler. When Jesus was warning the rich, He was not classifying people according to the amount of money they had. He was cautioning them about how attached they were to what they had.

You can be overly attached to your money and possessions whether you have just a meager amount or great wealth. Will your money become your blessing or your curse? Can money buy happiness? Can it buy contentment? Can it buy peace of mind?

Contrast the man of wealth in Mark 10 with the founder of the Quaker Oats Company, who gave 70% of his income to God. Or contrast the Chicago seven to Abraham, the wealthy father of many nations.

Abraham was not only a great man of faith, but also a very wealthy individual. Solomon was probably the richest man of his day. Barnabas, an early New Testament local church leader, was also wealthy but used his money and affluence to extend the kingdom of God.

James 5:1-3 speaks to the wealthy who use their money for personal gratification. James tells them they will weep and howl because of all the misery that is coming upon them. He boldly says that their gold and silver is plagued, and their precious metals will soon rust. James points out that it is foolish to value and esteem riches so highly that it causes corruption. It is harmless to possess riches, as long as the riches do not possess us.

Jesus recommended that we not stockpile our treasures in this life, at the expense of accumulating our treasures for the hereafter. In other words, if one is a long-term planner and visionary, it makes much more sense to accumulate wealth for the long haul in eternity. Time here on earth is the short haul; the temporary vapor of life. Life in eternity and life in heaven is the long-term commitment.

You own nothing and God owns everything. Whatever you have, God allowed you to accumulate. But when you die, how much of your money will you leave behind? All of it! When you die, how much of your money will you take with you? None of it!

Ultimately, you own nothing. You won't take your new BMW with you. You won't take those diamond rings or precious jewelry with you. You won't take your house with you. You won't take any property with you.

You won't take any of the possessions with you that you have managed to accumulate here on earth. You won't take your body because you don't own it. When your spirit leaves your body, it will return to dust.

Begin now to live a principled life. Determine at this moment to live the principle of appropriate use!

Principle 18

The Biblical Principle of Avoiding Overindulgence

f you plan to become debt free and stay that way for life, we need to address the subject of personal pleasure and overindulgence.

Proverbs 21:17

> *"He who loves pleasure will become poor; whoever loves wine and oil will never be rich."*

This verse tells us that loving pleasure and overindulgence squanders assets and prevents us from building proper financial resources.

Jesus said this in Luke 12:15, "Watch out! Be on your guard against all kinds of greed; a man's life does not consist in the abundance of his possessions."

In the United States, we live in a world filled with things and stuff. Revolving around things and stuff can be defined as materialism. Too often, our spending habits are built upon the foundation of materialism because we want things, and more things. We just can 't seem to get enough stuff.

Now hear me out. Having things is not the problem. Having the money to be able to purchase things is not the problem, but stuff and things should not be bought just because you have the money. Of course, if you don't have the money, they should not even be considered. As biblical stewards, we are not to spend the Master's money on things we don't need. That would be very foolish.

So if having wealth is not the problem, and having possessions is not the problem, then what is the obstacle, the potential stumbling block? The spiritual problem comes with the love of things. When we can't get enough, when we must have more, this is where we stumble spiritually.

Many parents attempt to express their love for their children by overindulgence in gifts and money. Perhaps this is their way of making up for being absentee parents, workaholic parents or for a lack of spiritual guidance in the family. But this contradicts many other biblical principles. The Christian way is all about servanthood and sacrifice, not materialism and overindulgence.

One definition of materialism states:

"The tendency to give undue importance to material interests; devotion to the material nature and its wants." The American Heritage® Dictionary of the English Language, Fourth Edition

Another definition of materialism:

"A desire for wealth and material possessions with little interest in ethical or spiritual matters." (*Webster's Revised Unabridged Dictionary*, © 1996, 1998 MICRA, Inc.)

A. W. Tozer said, "Never own anything; get rid of the sense of possessing!"

"Materialism is a view of life that regards the possession of material things as the highest good, the summum bonum. It involves more than a mere appreciation of physical things. It goes beyond the simple enjoyment of material benefits. This view is both radical and an ism. It is radical because it makes material things the heart or 'root' (radix) of all human happiness. It is an ism because it turns the neutral word 'material' into a philosophy of life." (Sproul, Jr., R. C. Biblical Economics. Tennessee: Draught Horse Press, 2002, p.23.)

Here is a biblical story about a fool and his possessions. He was even called a fool by God!

Luke 12:16-21

> *"And he told them this parable: 'The ground of a certain rich man produced a good crop. He thought to himself, What shall I do? I have no place to store my crops. Then he said, 'This is what I'll do. I will tear down my barns and build bigger ones, and there I will store all my grain and my goods. And I'll say to myself, You have plenty of good things laid up for many years. Take life easy; eat, drink and be merry.' But God said to him, 'You fool! This very night your life will be demanded from you. Then who will get what you have prepared for yourself?' This is how it will be with anyone who stores up things for himself but is not rich toward God."*

Well, what do YOU think? Was he a fool? Not many people have been so singled out by God. But before you jump on the bandwagon in agreement, read the story again. This story seems to be a picture of the American Dream!

The rich man was probably a hard and productive worker. He built and saved and toiled for a lifetime. This is not unlike some people today. They purchase their first little house, and when they outgrow it, they sell it and buy a bigger one. And when they get a little equity in the place, they place it on the market and look for a bigger, better, nicer, newer house!

The man in Luke 12 was shrewd. He was a builder; he was an investor. There is no evidence that he was dishonest, no evidence that he broke the law and no evidence that he evaded paying taxes. None whatsoever.

Some people today are just like him. They write best-selling books, give expensive seminars, have university buildings named after them and are proclaimed publicly as entrepreneurs – the individuals that make America great! They work hard, invest well and retire early.

Yet, in Luke 12, Jesus called this man a fool! Wow! Why?

Is it wrong to be successful? Is it wrong to have wealth? Does this mean that Christians should all be poor? No! Abraham, Isaac, Jacob,

Joseph, David, Solomon, Daniel, Joseph of Arimathea and Cornelius were all wealthy. Some of them, in fact, were extremely wealthy.

So what is the difference between the man called a fool by God and these great Old Testament patriarchs and New Testament characters? The difference is this: This man's outlook on life was totally self-centered. Everything he did was for himself. Every event, every purchase, every sale, everything was all about his personal ease and happiness. In his mind, HE, not God, was the sole owner of his life and his possessions. And his priorities – they were so badly skewed that he deserved the tag "fool."

He used his wealth for himself rather than for the kingdom of God. His security was all wrapped up in his ability, his money and his possessions. He was headed for a retirement life of ease, but one without God. A retirement of self-serving gratification, not a retirement of servanthood.

Yes, it's true that the Abrahams, Isaacs, Jacobs, Josephs, Davids, Solomons and Daniels of the Bible were rich. But here is the difference between them and the Luke 12 fool. They had wealth, but each of them was totally devoted to God.

Is it wrong to enjoy the blessing of God? Of course not, but the blessing of God does mean we must have our priorities right in life. First, God must be recognized as the source of all things. Second, He must be credited with full ownership of all we possess. Third, it must be known that our spiritual prosperity is infinitely more important than our material prosperity.

3 John 2

> *"Beloved, I pray that you may prosper in all things and be in health, just as your soul prospers" (NKJV).*

Joshua 1:8

> *"Do not let this Book of the Law depart from your mouth; meditate on it day and night, so that you may be careful to do everything written in it. Then you will be prosperous and successful."*

Begin now to live a principled life. Determine at this moment to live the principle of avoiding overindulgence!

Principle 19

The Biblical Principle of Financial Diligence

Proverbs 10:4, 5

> *"Lazy hands make a man poor, but diligent hands bring wealth. He who gathers crops in summer is a wise son, but he who sleeps during harvest is a disgraceful son."*

Becoming debt free and remaining debt free requires financial diligence. Nothing can be accomplished without meticulousness in your economic life. As the Scripture says, lazy hands lead to poverty, but attentiveness to good work habits and good financial habits can lead to prosperity and success.

Some people today would rather ask for a handout instead of going to work. You see them waiting at the freeway exits holding signs that read, "will work for food." After offering one person a day's work in exchange for wages, his response was nothing more than profanity and gestures. The integrity of this person was certainly lacking and his honesty brought into full question.

A person's usefulness is determined to a great degree by his motivation to work. Idleness is not looked upon kindly in biblical passages nor within our society today.

The Bible is clear about the principle of working diligently. It says that a lazy person who conveniently excuses himself from working with a little sleep, a little slumber, and a little folding of the hands to rest will come to naught. His life will be one of poverty, bankruptcy and uselessness. He is one who consoles himself with rest, unconcerned that others are getting the job done.

The person who does not work diligently is nothing short of lazy. However, the person who gets up early, gets right to work and prepares for the future, will someday be honored for it. Proverbs 22:29 points this out by saying, "Do you see a man who excels in his work? He will stand before kings" (NKJV).

Hebrews 6:10, 11

> *"God is not unjust; he will not forget your work and the love you have shown him as you have helped his people and continue to help them. We want each of you to show this same diligence to the very end, in order to make your hope sure."*

From this scripture, we can clearly see that diligence produces the fruit of what you hope for. If you commit to working diligently, God says He will not forget what you have done and will, in turn, reward you.

Colossians 3:23

> *"Whatever you do, work at it with all your heart, as working for the LORD, not for men."*

This passage tells believers they must be diligent and focused on whatever God is asking them to do. That not only applies to a job, but also to finances. Finances are, of course, directly linked to your job – that's what brings in the cash! Diligence and hard work are simply part of the Christian walk.

Begin now to live a principled life. Determine at this moment to live the principle of financial diligence!

Principle 20

The Biblical Principle of Fiscal Planning

Proverbs 21:5

> *"The plans of the diligent lead surely to advantage, but everyone who is hasty comes surely to poverty" (NASB).*

The shrewd person looks ahead and plans for the future. He manages money so as to provide benefit not only for the present, but also for future financial reward. William Jennings Bryan (1860 – 1925) noted, "Destiny is not a matter of chance, it is a matter of choice."

What is involved in the planning process? Planning is outlining a course of action now in order to achieve a financial goal, thus fulfilling a desired objective. It is predetermining today a course of action for tomorrow. It is throwing a net over tomorrow and making something happen. It is being tomorrow minded rather than yesterday minded.

The only way to reach a financial goal is to work at it. The most important step in reaching the goal is to develop a plan to achieve it. That's why it is important to plan ahead for your retirement and your financial future.

The idea of planning ahead and building a solid financial strategy for success can sometimes be intimidating and feel a little overwhelming, but once you get started it will become easier for you.

With a little planning and a better understanding of what your investment options are, you too can successfully manage your money and pursue your financial goals. So what is planning? Planning is knowing where you are today, outlining the steps it will take to reach your financial goals, developing a sound plan, and continuing to follow the pattern you outlined by pursuing your goals.

Planning involves measurement and feedback. Planning is being decisive and doing work today designed to cause specified occurrences tomorrow.

"I urge you to plan your work and then work your plan. I urge you to let no obstacle get in your way of accomplishing your plan. Either go around it, over it, or through it. But don't turn around and go back. You do not retreat. You do not quit." –Alan N. Canton

The principle of financial planning is important. Take time to plan for your financial future. Good planning is an essential step toward meeting your financial goals. Plans must be flexible. They must be evaluated. They must be revised from time to time. Don't delay, get started today!

Begin now to live a principled life. Determine at this moment to live the principle of fiscal planning!

Principle 21

The Biblical Principle of Tomorrow Thinking

2 Chronicles 26:5

"As long as he sought the Lord, God gave him success."

Proverbs 21:5

"The plans of the diligent lead surely to advantage, but everyone who is hasty comes surely to poverty" (NASB).

Retirement Planning

Financial security does not just happen. It takes a lot of planning, a heavy dose of commitment and money. It is a fact, according to government statistics, that less than half of Americans have put aside money specifically for retirement. One third of those who have 401(k) coverage available to them do not participate in the plan.

You can't retire with security unless your really prepare for it. This means facing up to reality, and beginning to take action for tomorrow as well as today. Putting away money for retirement is like giving yourself a raise. It's money that gives you freedom when you want it and when you deserve it.

Increasing numbers of people are finding that retirement is staring them in the face before they are ready to leave the work force. The jobs they had counted on to sustain them in their later years may have been a victim of company layoffs.

Many are facing employment that pays less, but more significant, the loss of pension or retirement plans they thought would be theirs. It is important to invest personal money and adequately prepare for the golden years.

Retirement planning is taking on greater importance these days, as more and more people face involuntary termination because of changes in corporate downsizing and the American economy.

Know your retirement needs. Retirement living is expensive. How much are you saving for the future? Most financial planners recommend you save 10 to 15% of your income. But many of us fall short of that goal. How much will you need to retire? How much will you need to save by the time you are 62, 65 or 66?

Experts estimate you will need at least 70% of your pre-retirement income to maintain your standard of living. If you are not making a moderately good living now, you may need as much as 90% of your current income to live comfortably in your retirement years.

Know your future financial needs. According to the government figures on aging, only one-third of people currently employed have attempted to learn how much they must save to achieve a comfortable retirement. Of those who have investigated it, still 42% remain unsure how much money they will need to save to retire. How much money do you need for retirement?

The answer depends on the lifestyle you foresee during retirement. It depends on how long you live and how long your family members historically have lived. The answer to this also depends on your retirement goals. Do you plan to travel around the world? Do you plan to live just as you do now? How much money will you be leaving to your heirs?

Some expenses will decrease as a result of your age. You won't be paying Social Security taxes, work expenses or contributing to retirement plans. However, some expenses, such as health care and travel, may increase dramatically.

Know your housing needs. Most older people prefer to remain in their own homes during their later years, even if it means some remodeling to accommodate their health concerns. Even when frail and vulnerable, or when afflicted with a chronic illness, people want to stay in familiar surroundings.

This can mean hiring expensive health-care professionals to come into their homes to provide proper care. Often this is not possible when people have failed to save enough to meet such needs. Adequate income and assets are critically important to enable well being in virtually all dimensions of life in our later years.

Know your health needs. A wealth of information is available about maintaining physical and mental health, as well as achieving an adequate level of economic security to remain as independent as possible. You can live an active and productive life and enjoy retirement.

The longevity of life provides new opportunities for our retirement years. The aging of the American population presents both new challenges and new opportunities. Of course, this also heaps more responsibility upon us to prepare for that lengthened life span. As a result, our retirement plans must address special needs.

Saving for Retirement – Young and Old

Whether you are close to retirement or many years away, it is never too early or too late to plan for retirement. You control your financial future by identifying your retirement needs, setting money aside, and making wise investment decisions now. Tell some young family to start now to prepare for retirement and they stare in disbelief. They think they are still young and have lots of time before they need to save for retirement.

The earlier a family starts, the more they will be able to salt away some great savings. That is because time is money and the power of compound interest is enormous. Assume you want to build a $100,000 nest egg by age 65 and that you can earn 10% on your money.

You need to contribute only $16 per month if you start saving at age 25. If you wait till you're 35, you need to contribute $44 per month. The necessary contribution rises to $131 per month if you wait till 45, and skyrockets to $484 per month if you wait till 55.

Here is another example. Suppose you are a young person 20 years old. You start saving or investing just $21.60 each week and attain an average of 10% on your investment over a 45-year period. By the time you reach the retirement age of 65, your account would be worth $1,000,802.11. More than one million dollars! This shows the power of investing just a little bit over the long haul.

Investment Detail
*Interest Rate Compounded Continuously
*Weekly Payment Made at Beginning of the Period
*45 Years / 2,340 Weekly Payments of $21.60
*Interest Rate of 10%
*Total Contributions: $50,544

On the other hand, some older couples excuse their lack of saving by thinking they are too old to start saving for retirement. Although it is true you can't make up for lost time and opportunity, it's never too late to start saving. Someone who takes early retirement at age 55 may still be going strong 30 years later. You'll have to contribute more to your retirement savings account than if you started it decades ago, but the time to start saving seriously is now.

No one actively plans to fail in providing for a comfortable old age. We simply fail to plan. Our grandparents faced different problems with money than we do. They were frightened by bank failures and the depression and tended to put their money into just three places – a home, a bank and insurance.

Today we have to be prepared for the havoc that inflation can play on our investments over the long term, as well as corporate fraud or an up and down economy. No one actively plans to fail in providing for a comfortable old age. We simply fail to plan.

Begin now to live a principled life. Determine at this moment to live the principle of tomorrow thinking!

Principle 22

The Biblical Principle of Economic Rewards

Jeremiah 17:10

> *"I the* Lord *search the heart and examine the mind, to reward a man according to his conduct, according to what his deeds deserve."*

Matthew 16:27

> *"He will reward each person according to what he has done."*

All actions have their reward. Whether good or bad, temporary or eternal, rewards come as a result of our action. Often we predetermine our reward by predetermining our actions. But, of course, it all takes action on our part. How about your language skills? Could they use some improvement? Do you wish you had a bigger vocabulary but can never find the time to do a lot of studying?

Suppose you could carve 10 minutes out of every day (during TV commercials?) and you used that time to learn a new word. In 25 years you would have learned 9,125 words! This would be a nice reward indeed! The point is a simple one. The small changes we make in our lives can have a significant effect if maintained over a long period of time.

Sometimes our rewards come as a result of our actions that begin with New Year's resolutions. Most resolutions are started in the first few months of the year. We might want to lose weight, eat healthy, exercise or even get out of debt. Those are all worthwhile goals.

Most of us get frustrated trying to reach something that's too big. We just can't picture ourselves being 40 or 50 pounds lighter. In fact we won't lose that much weight in a short time even if we go on an all-out crash diet. The majority of people put the pounds right back on after they finish their diets.

Those who are successful follow a different approach. They change their lifestyle just a little bit, but only as much change as they're willing to accept on an ongoing basis. Maybe they cut out one soda per day –or add 15 minutes of exercise per day, something they can sustain for years to come.

Will they lose the 40 pounds? Not all at once. But they will begin to lose a pound or two each month. After a couple of years they will have achieved their goal and also given themselves a healthier lifestyle.

What is the lesson to be learned here? There are two. The first is that you don't need to be afraid to dream big. You can accomplish big things without doing anything heroic or noteworthy.

Financial Rewards

The second lesson? Take small and determined steps toward your goal. Save a few dollars each and every week. Not a lot one week and none the next, but a few dollars each week.

Make regular progress to your ultimate destination a habit. If you fail one day, get right back on track. You won't go far in any one day, but you will cover a lot of ground over time.

On the other hand, you can decide that you don't want to make the small changes. Maybe you will be the one in 37 million who hits the lottery. But it's much more likely that you'll just be swimming upstream your whole life.

So how does that apply to our financial lives? Let's take a look at another natural occurrence. One thing we notice in nature is that many things start small and take time to grow. But they can grow to a large size if enough time passes.

Trees are an excellent example. They start from a seed, acorn or sapling and can grow to be hundreds of feet high.

The same thing can happen with our finances. Consider borrowing money. Suppose you spent $10 more than you make each week. And you continue to do that every week for 50 years. Remember that $10 isn't a large amount to borrow each week. But if you do that continually and pay only a fairly good rate of interest (10% annually) you'll owe more than $762,000 after 50 years.

Of course, it works the same in the other direction. If you saved $10 a week you'd be a millionaire in the 52nd year of your program. So it really doesn't take a big shift to move you from serious debt to being comfortable financially.

Okay, I can hear some of you saying that you'd have a tough time saving $10 per week. Could you save 72 cents a day? That's $5 a week. In just 30 years you'd have a bit less than $50,000. Again, a small change in direction can make a major difference.

Saving Rewards

You can receive financial rewards by saving and by personal discipline! It isn't easy to save! It takes a commitment to start saving and sticking to it. Something else will always be waiting to take your money. But no one else will save for you, so you have to do it for yourself.

You may have heard that "a penny saved is a penny earned." But actually a penny saved is more than a penny earned. This is especially true if you invest it in an IRA or retirement plan. If your pennies earn a 7% interest rate, then the following applies:

In 10 years, 1,000 pennies, or $10 a week, would grow to $7,185. In 20 years, 1,000 pennies, or $10 a week, would grow to $21,318. In 30 years, 1,000 pennies, or $10 a week, would grow to $49,120.

A financial reward is waiting for you when you save. But, of course, your prearranged action predetermines the extent of that financial reward. How much and when you begin makes a difference in the amount of the reward.

When should you begin? As early as you can. If you start at 25, and put away $25 a month, you could reach $300,000 by age 65. If you wait until 45, that $300,000 at 65 may cost $300 a month.

Remember the rule of 72. This tells you how long it will take to double your money at a given rate of interest. You simply divide 72 by the interest your money is earning. At 6%, your savings will double in 12 years. At 9%, they will double in eight years.

Year after year, any money you invest may earn interest, dividends or capital gains. When you reinvest those earnings, they help generate additional earnings; those additional earnings help generate more earnings, and so on. This is called compounding. For example, if an investment returns 8% a year and its earnings are reinvested annually:

- After one year, your total return will be 8%.
- After five years, your cumulative total return will be 47%.
- After ten years, your cumulative total return will be 116%.

Remember that the financial reward may not be of the greatest importance to all. Other rewards can play an even greater role.

Thomas Edison was one such person in which another reward was greater. He said, "One might think that the money value of an invention constitutes its reward to the man who loves his work. But speaking for myself, I can honestly say this is not so . . . . I continue to find my greatest pleasure, and so my reward, in the work that precedes what the world calls success." (1847-1931)

John Ruskin weighed in with this word, "The highest reward for a person's toil is not what they get for it, but what they become by it." (1819-1900)

Begin now to live a principled life. Determine at this moment to live the principle of economic rewards!

Principle 23

The Biblical Principle of Being Debt Free

Romans 13:7, 8

> *"Pay everyone whatever he ought to have: pay your taxes and import duties gladly, obey those over you, and give honor and respect to all those to whom it is due. Pay all your debts except the debt of love for others– never finish paying that!" (TLB).*

The Scripture is clear about the benefits of being a lender as opposed to being the borrower. Clearly, being the lender is preferred. Of course, you can never enjoy being in that position unless you have become debt free yourself.

Shakespeare said, "Neither a borrower or lender be, For loan oft loses both itself and friend, and borrowing dulls the edge of husbandry." (1564 – 1616)

The relative ease of obtaining credit enables consumers to get goods and services when cash is not readily available. It also allows them to buy things on sale, make purchases when prices are low, and pay for items at the same time they are using and enjoying them.

Unfortunately, problems and financial risks occur because consumers and creditors abuse credit. Careless use of credit can lead to financial difficulty, family problems, repossession of property, garnishment of wages and even bankruptcy. The bottom line is this: If you don't borrow money, you can't get into debt.

Options are available to help you manage financial difficulties when bills stack up and you cannot pay them. This topic discusses how to spot potential debt problems, how to set up a debt-payment plan, and court provisions for handling credit obligations.

Many people find themselves deep in debt at least once in their lifetimes. It is not necessarily brought on by a desire to spend oneself into oblivion, but rather by a lack of family financial planning. In this section, I list 15 steps one can follow to get out of debt. This should help fight the debt mountain.

Some of my friends who are snow skiers can't understand why I am not excited about joining them on ski trips to Mt. Hood. I grew up in the Midwest where 20 degrees below zero and annual snowfalls of well over 100 inches took all the excitement and anticipation out of the winter months. Yet my friends continue to tell me that gliding down the slopes is exhilarating and that there's nothing like it.

Skiing into debt is also exciting. However, the price of escaping from the debt is greater than most people realize. Simply stopping the intake of new debt is not enough. A multiple financial reverse is involved. Look at what must happen to work out of the debt trap.

- Stop spending more than is earned.
- Spend considerably less than before.
- Pay the oldest debt.
- Pay the interest on the debt.

Your journey to financial freedom will be an individual one. Your own circumstances will have a lot to say about your plan. The following steps are a guide to map your own course.

- Decide to change.
- Determine not to overspend.
- Spend much less than you make.
- Do not add any new debts.
- Pay with cash.
- Determine what you owe.
- Prioritize your debt.
- Determine how much you can pay.
- Create a payoff plan.
- Communicate with your creditors.
- Establish a repayment timeline.

- Reduce your timeline with all extra monies.
- Stay focused on your plan.
- Stay with your plan.
- Seek professional counsel as needed.

Begin now to live a principled life. Determine at this moment to live the principle of being debt free!

Principle 24

The Biblical Principle of Not Borrowing Money

"Just as the rich rule the poor, so the borrower is servant to the lender" (Proverbs 22:7, TLB).

This scripture and others like it show us who is really calling the shots when it comes to money. The "haves" rule the "have nots" (i.e. the borrower is the servant to the lender). Yet in spite of this biblical reality, the debt-ridden consumer continues to borrow even more money without regard to the consequences.

There is a great danger in our society of getting trapped by debt. With this principle I want to address a number of borrowing and credit issues. Perhaps the greatest need in families today is understanding the consequences of being trapped by debt with limited income and in a financial position where it seems like it will be impossible to recover.

Any person can find a wealth of information that focuses on borrowing, easy credit and debt issues, but the problem I have found in counseling is failing to get a person(s) to recognize the seriousness of their actions before they make wrong decisions.

All to often, people only want help after their situation has become nearly hopeless. Just know that borrowing can be very hazardous to your financial health and possibly to your mental health, spiritual health and the health of your relationships.

Much of borrowing done by a person today is for short-term loans. But for the most part this kind of credit goes to purchase things that generally have no asset value associated with it. Usually this has more to do with our wants and desires than our actual needs. Unfortunately, long after the item purchased is consumed, the debt repayment goes on.

Mark Twain had a couple of significant things to say about credit. "Beautiful credit! The foundation of modern society. Who shall say that this is not the golden age of mutual trust, of unlimited reliance upon human promises? That is a peculiar condition of society which enables a whole nation to instantly recognize point and meaning in the familiar newspaper anecdote, which puts into the mouth of a distinguished speculator in lands and mines this remark: 'I wasn't worth a cent two years ago, and now I owe two millions of dollars.'"

Too often families are quick to borrow instead of trusting the Lord to meet their needs. After all, does not Scripture tell us that our God is a providing God; that He will take care of us by meeting out needs? What if we turn to credit and take on new debt, when all along God wanted to show Himself strong on our behalf. Before you run to the bank for a loan, before you pull out the charge card, before you rush to meet your own needs, give time for the provision of God to work.

Philippians 4:17-19

> *"Not that I am looking for a gift, but I am looking for what may be credited to your account. I have received full payment and even more; I am amply supplied, now that I have received from Epaphroditus the gifts you sent. They are a fragrant offering, an acceptable sacrifice, pleasing to God. And my God will meet all your needs according to his glorious riches in Christ Jesus."*

Because we have been taught from childhood to make our own way, to make decisions, and to move quickly and decisively, we hurry to fix our own problems. While we are not to be slow to work, we should be slow in waiting on God. We should be slow in always making our own way independently of seeking the wisdom of God.

Isaiah 55:7-9

> *"Let the wicked forsake his way and the evil man his thoughts. Let him turn to the LORD, and He will have mercy on him, and to our God, for He will freely pardon, ... For my thoughts are not your thoughts, neither are your ways my ways," declares the LORD. "As the heavens are higher than the earth, so are my ways higher than your ways and my thoughts than your thoughts."*

Borrow Money as a Last Resort

Loan consolidation, home equity loans, or refinancing your home are ways to avoid repossession or loss of income through wage garnishment. These options may reduce the amount of your monthly payment. However, the cost for borrowing is usually increased, because the borrowing time is extended and you may be borrowing at a higher interest rate. If you can manage to pay your debts without loan consolidation, home equity loans, or refinancing, you probably will save yourself extra expense.

The use of these options generally do not improve poor money management habits, and the reduced monthly payment may encourage you to acquire more debts.

Getting into Debt Is Simple

The road into the misuse of credit is wide, broad, simple, easy, accessible, effortless, uncomplicated, painless, spacious, available and trouble free. However, there is no quick and easy way out from under a heavy debt load. With debt, in essence, you slide in and climb out – easy to get in, difficult to get out.

If you have ever been heavily in debt and burdened down with monthly payments so steep that you could barely keep your head above water, and then had to slowly and methodically climb out, you know what I am talking about. It is an uphill struggle. There is no easy way out. I cannot wave a magic wand and help you undo in 12 months what it took 12 years to accomplish.

The Lifestyle of Debt

What about a lifestyle of debt? Is a Christian to borrow? Is debt okay? Some would believe it is wrong for a Christian to have any debt. Some will say it is all right to borrow for a house, but never borrow for anything that would depreciate. While I am not in that camp, I do believe that one of the greatest challenges and hindrances to reaching the world for Christ is that people who live in a society where there is the possibility of making significant amounts of money, all to often, spend their way into enormous debt. In doing so, there is little left over above their tithing to give to their local church missions and evangelism projects. If you have to borrow, learn to give while borrowing.

Borrow Money with the Right Intentions

It is not wrong to borrow money, but it is wrong to take on debt without the ability to pay it back or with the intention of never repaying what is owed. What is meant in Romans 13:8 when it says not to owe anything to anyone?

"Obey the laws, then, for two reasons: first, to keep from being punished, and second, just because you know you should. Pay your taxes too, for these same two reasons. For government workers need to be paid so that they can keep on doing God's work, serving you. Pay everyone whatever he ought to have: pay your taxes and import duties gladly, obey those over you, and give honor and respect to all those to whom it is due. Pay all your debts except the debt of love for others – never finish paying that! For if you love them, you will be obeying all of God's laws, fulfilling all his requirements" (Romans 13:5-8; TLB).

These verses simply mean that you should obey the laws, pay your taxes and repay all of your debts. That just makes good sense. But more than repaying your debts at some future date, you are to pay your creditors on time with interest owed. A person who borrows but does not repay is called wicked, meaning wrong, sinful, immoral, evil and depraved.

Psalm 37:21

"The wicked borrow and do not repay, but the righteous give generously."

Live a Self-controlled Lifestyle

If a person or family will live a restrained lifestyle, they will be able to live on thousands of dollars less each year. You should incur debt only when it makes good economic sense. The expense of borrowing should be less than the economic benefit you will receive.

Don't underestimate the interest of God to help you in every way. Over and over the Scriptures indicate that you are to live a controlled and temperate lifestyle.

> *"Now the overseer must be above reproach . . . temperate, self-controlled, respectable" (I Timothy 3:2).*

> *"Thus says the LORD, your Redeemer, the Holy One of Israel: 'I am the LORD your God, who teaches you to profit, who leads you by the way you should go'" (Isaiah 48:17; NKJV).*

The Problem of Easy Credit

The problem with easy credit is that banking institutions are always willing to give you more money than you have the ability to repay. If you need to borrow a thousand dollars for an unexpected need because you have not set aside dollars for that purpose, the lending institutions will try to give you several thousand more than you actually need. While at first blush that may give you great pride and confidence thinking that someone really believes in you, in reality the only way a bank makes money is to make loans.

If you receive seven or eight thousand dollars and you only needed one thousand, rest assured you will find a way to spend the extra. It will disappear without you knowing where it went. The less you borrow the less you pay back and the more you have available to give to missions and the needs of others. Credit should always be the exception and not the rule.

One of the problems with obtaining credit is that you are presuming nothing is going to change for the worse in the future. You are assuming you and your spouse will have adequate income for repayment, that your jobs are secure and that your income stream will be the same or more in later years.

There is a danger in making assumptions. It could be that your intended source of repayment changes. Jobs are lost, the value of stocks and bonds can decline or even disappear, assets may not appreciate as quickly as anticipated or they might even lose their value.

> *"Now listen, you who say, 'Today or tomorrow we will go to this or that city, spend a year there, carry on business and make money.' Why, you do not even know what will happen tomorrow. What is your life? You are a mist that appears for a little while and then vanishes. Instead, you ought to say, 'If it is the LORD's will, we will live and do this or that'" (James 4:13-15).*

The Bondage of Debt

Show me a person deep in debt and I'll show you a person who feels in bondage. You are so burdened down with the heavy load of debt, it is like becoming a servant to your creditors. You work all day for days on end just to meet your payment obligations to your debtors. You gladly volunteer for all the overtime you can get, work a part-time job in the evenings or on weekends, all for the purpose of getting a larger paycheck so you can turn it over to someone else. Well, all this is not breaking news. You knew about it long before you borrowed the money. You read about it in Scripture.

> *"The rich rule over the poor, and the borrower is servant to the lender" (Proverbs 22:7).*

Is Credit Debt Dangerous?

Americans are two trillion dollars in debt. Credit, the ability to borrow money, can be very dangerous. In short, it's spending money today that will be tomorrow's income. Most economists would say that credit is an important part of the ability of individuals, families, cities and ultimately nations to function in a financial world. Credit consists of unpaid balances on auto loans, credit cards, student loans and generally any non-mortgage debt.

One of the real dangers of excessive borrowing is that it creates high monthly payments, which often strains even well planned budgets. The pace of borrowing often exceeds the family's growth in income and leads to a form of "credit debt bondage." The interest expense of credit debt is often very high. Banks and other lending institutions often will loan to people with a higher credit risk, but do so at the expense of the borrower.

When employed by a major national bank as a Vice President and Business Banking Officer, I learned of a huge profit opportunity for the company. Often those that did not qualify for the terms of a regular loan could still get money, but at an interest rate several points higher than normal. Of course, individuals, families and businesses would quickly agree because, in reality, they needed the money at any cost.

People that have high monthly credit payments often sacrifice their other financial goals just to make their payments. This is a very serious offense. By not investing in a house, savings account or other forms of investment, they seriously put their future retirement in question.

Excessive debt cannot be ignored. It will not go away. You can ignore past due bills, but you do so at the risk of finding yourself in even worse circumstances. A chain of events are triggered when you do not pay your bills. Creditors can take action against you, the past due bills can be turned over to a debt collector, your property can be repossessed, your wages garnished, and so on.

While debt bondage is the result of unwise decisions and excess credit purchases, there is no easy way out. The reason people find themselves in this position is that they spend more than they earned and the only way out is to spend less and pay the difference on their debt balance. The only way out of this dangerous situation is to be in control of their spending and put themselves on a budget, which is just a written plan that provides oversight and guidance to their spending habits.

Secrets of Borrowing Less

It is always wise to borrow less than more. Cultivate the mindset that you will borrow only for absolute necessities, and that you will repay the loan at the earliest possible date. Paying back a larger amount than the required fixed payment will help you retire the debt early. For what things should you not be getting a loan and for what would you borrow? In general, it all depends on your ability to repay the loan within a practical period of time.

While you could obtain credit to purchase an asset with reasonable potential to gain in value, you should not borrow for something that will continue to lose its value from the moment you buy it. Another sensible cause to borrow money would be for something obtained that would bring you income opportunity. If you have a skill or a trade and a particular tool or machine that would generate additional income, then credit might be a possibility to explore.

Pledge Yourself to Delayed Gratification

Don't get in the habit of buying something before you need it or because you think you might use it at some future date. Indulgence because you think you "owe it to yourself" or "it will help your self-esteem" is a bad habit.

You can develop habits that will ensure you will enjoy financial success, regardless of how much or how little your income. Many earn very little over a lifetime, yet manage to save enough for a debt free and secure retirement.

Credit Card Debt and Interest

Your current credit card debt represents more than just the fact that you owe money. It represents the fact that you are spending more money than you are making. It represents the fact that you are out of touch with your financial future. It represents the fact that you need to attend to this now – or it will likely get worse before it gets better.

A few years ago I was preparing my taxes, and had been waiting for my interest statement paid to the only Visa card I have. In that particular year, I charged $26,000 on my credit card so I wanted to know my interest amount. So I called the card issuer and was told I had paid zero interest that year. In disbelief, I went back through each statement and found it was true.

The lesson here; if you are going to have a credit card, use it for convenience and pay it off in full at the time of each statement. If you cannot do that, you have no business carrying a card with you – pay cash instead.

Record nickels and dimes spent for the past 90 days and the next 90 days. If you don't know where the money went, how can you get out of debt? Close your eyes and visualize a stress-free, debt-free lifestyle. You are on vacation, but you have paid it all in advance. It is not more income you need; it is less spending.

Scripture says the poor will always be with us, but it does not say none of them will be Christians. A friend of mine, who is very brilliant individual, once made a statement that seemed very odd to me. He said, "I cannot understand why God has not made me rich yet." I have no magic formulas, but this one. Live within, not above, your income!

I have a friend who had purchased a couple of fine houses, but then sold them to pay off his debt, only to get into debt all over again. It is more important that I teach you why you should stay out of debt than to teach you how to get out of debt.

Let me settle something for you right now. You will never win the lottery so quit spending money on tickets. Quit spending money as if you were about to win the lottery. God's ways are not about windfall income like the lottery. His ways are about thriftiness, staying out of debt, working hard and serving Him. How do we get out of debt? Just the way we got into debt – one step at a time.

If you give a man a fish you can feed him for a day. If you teach him to fish, you can feed him for life. It's not going to help you one bit if I major on how to get out of debt. The real help comes if I can change your attitude that causes you to move from a lifestyle of debt to the freedom of being debt free and becoming financially independent.

Deuteronomy 28:43-45

> *"The alien who lives among you will rise above you higher and higher, but you will sink lower and lower. He will lend to you, but you will not lend to him. He will be the head, but you will be the tail."*

How Can I Get Help?

First go to God in repentance and ask forgiveness for mishandling that which He has entrusted to you. Remember that in your borrowing, you promised to repay. In essence, you made a vow when you incurred debt. Borrowing or lending, for that matter, is not necessarily wrong or prohibited in Scripture, but it is discouraged in a number of Scriptures.

When you get into trouble because of your own unwise choices and bad decisions, while God will help you find a way out, it will not be at the expense of defrauding those to whom you go. Forgiveness is always available, but the consequences of our wrong actions remain.

Luke 11:9, 10

> *"So I say to you: Ask and it will be given to you; seek and you will find; knock and the door will be opened to you. For everyone who asks receives; he who seeks finds; and to him who knocks, the door will be opened."*

In order to borrow at competitive rates it is important to be a credit-worthy person. Everyone knows that potential lenders look closely at your credit record, but did you also know that landLords and insurance companies do, too? Here are some tips for building up a clean credit record – and making sure it stays that way.

You probably already know that your credit report is all-important when it comes to qualifying for any type of loan, including a mortgage, an auto loan, or a low-rate credit card. But you may not realize that having a lousy credit rating (or credit score, which I'll talk about in a minute) can impede you when it comes to getting a job, renting an apartment or even getting a decent rate on auto insurance.

Landlords, employers and insurance companies have all discovered that someone who pays bills on time is likely to be responsible enough to pay them as well, and responsible enough to drive safely on the roads. That means it's in your best interest to keep your credit report – and your credit score – in its best possible condition.

Now you probably know that your credit report is essentially your credit history. It details what sort of loans are outstanding, how long you've had them, whether you pay your bills on time and so on (the information is not just from credit card companies, but all your creditors, including utilities, landLORDS, hospitals, banks, etc.).

Your credit score, however, is more complicated. It's a computer-based determination of the risk you pose to each of your creditors. In fact, it's calculated differently for each lender, using those particular parts of your credit report that are thought to be the most telling.

According to Fair, Isaac & Co., a leading supplier of credit data, these scores include up to 100 factors, including the number of times you've paid bills 60 days late, the size of your credit line (particularly the part that isn't being used), the number of recent inquiries into your credit history (an indication that you're looking for more credit) and any bankruptcies, liens and foreclosures.

Unfortunately, while you can, and should, take an annual look at your credit report, you can't see your credit score. It's available only to lenders and they pay handsomely for it. But you improve your score (and your overall credit history) with some fairly simple maneuvers, which I will cover later.

Begin now to live a principled life. Determine at this moment to live the principle of not borrowing money!

Principle 25

The Biblical Principle of Financial Discipline

Hebrews 12:11

> *"No discipline seems pleasant at the time, but painful. Later on, however, it produces a harvest of . . . peace for those who have been trained by it."*

Financial discipline is the ability to handle money in a responsible manner. The Bible indicates that control of finances in one's possession is a direct indication of the control exercised in spiritual matters. If a person cannot handle God's blessing of finance, it is likely he cannot handle too much time on his hands, promotion on the job, authority on the job, authority in the church, and probably a whole host of other spiritual and natural issues.

The "unjust steward" of Luke 16 had other personal problems besides just being a bad manager for his Lord. His dishonesty became very apparent when he was about to lose his job. The handling of a person's financial affairs is similar to his / her other values. The value system of one's heart is exposed by his relationship to money and material things. The rich young ruler is another illustration of that fact (See Matthew 19:16-22).

The biblical principle of financial discipline cannot be ignored. Ignoring that principle allowed you to get into debt in the first place. While staying out of debt is not so easy, getting out of debt once you are in debt is very difficult. Benjamin Franklin said, "Creditors have better memories than debtors."

Before you can become debt free, you must assess just where you are. How much in debt are you? What kind of debt do you have? What can you do to perform a financial checkup? What information will you need to gather? Are you headed for serious financial trouble? All these questions need to be answered before you can get on the right road to financial recovery. Two Chinese proverbs are applicable here: "A good debt is not as good as no debt," and "Free from debt is free from care."

Check Your Financial Well-Being

So what's the quickest way to check your financial well being? If you don't like accounting, math, and bank statements, you've probably never really taken your financial temperature. But is there a fast and painless way to get a feel for whether you're in financial trouble?

Yes, there are a couple of techniques that you can use. Obviously, they're not going to give you as much information as if you took the time to do a personal balance sheet and budget, but they will let you know if you're heading for serious financial trouble. Let's spend some time giving you a financial checkup to see the condition of your financial health.

Checkbook

One way is to look at your checkbook. If I were to ask to see all your cancelled checks and credit card statements for the past 12 months, what would that tell me about you and your spending habits?

One biographer said that when he started to do research on a person, the first thing he wanted to know was how that person spent money. He felt that if he could look at the checkbook he'd learn more about that person than if he went to interview friends and relatives.

We can learn a lot about ourselves in the same way. What's the biggest check you wrote last month? If you still have a mortgage, that should be it. If the biggest check went somewhere else, you might want to ask yourself "why?"

Paying for college is expensive and may demand a rather high monthly payment. But if your car payment is as high you could be heading for trouble financially.

Maybe you don't have a mortgage payment. Perhaps you're elderly and have already paid it off. If so, the biggest check each month should be written to your retirement saving account. Or are you taking that money and using it to pay for a boat or other luxury instead?

Look at the other big checks you write. How many of them are to pay monthly bills for things you bought long ago? Are you still paying for the furniture that's been in your living room for three years? What about TV's, stereos and electronics? Making monthly payments on those types of items is a danger sign.

Now let's do a little rough math. Look at your deposits for the month. Then compare those big unavoidable monthly bills, you know, your mortgage, car payments and utilities. Do those payments consume more than two-thirds of your deposits? If so, you are already in dangerous territory. A closer look is in order.

Don't forget about the little checks either. Are you writing a lot of small checks to credit card companies? How are you recording your credit card purchases? Are you deducting from your check register each time you make a credit card purchase?

Maybe you're spending too much time in the mall. What about checks for cash or ATM transactions? Are you always just a little short of cash? If so, it may be time to look at some of that "miscellaneous" spending. Those 5 and 10 dollar lunches can add up over time.

What about your credit card bills? Are you among the 30% who pay off all their purchases every month? If so, you probably have your spending under control.

Credit Card Statements

Look at your credit card statements. Can you remember what you bought with each charge? If you can't remember what you bought, there's a good chance you didn't need it.

Think about all the ones you do remember. Were you buying things you really needed? Or was it for something you just wanted at the time? Have you used all those things since you bought them?

Here's a quick test for you. Are you just paying the minimum each month on your credit card account? Flash the warning lights! Look at it this way. For every $1,000 you owe on your account you may be paying up to $200 each year in interest payments.

Feelings about Money

If you have a credit card balance of $5,000, that comes to about $100 in interest every month that doesn't bring any food, clothing or anything else into your house. Do your own math to see how much is flying out your window every month in interest. Wouldn't you rather have no credit card balance? Wouldn't you rather be debt free?

Finally, how do you feel about money? Some people look at money as a vehicle to have some fun and base their happiness on the amount of fun money can bring to them. They think they can buy things and happiness will follow. Those are usually the people with large credit card bills.

Others view money as a measure of their success. They need to earn more than their neighbor to feel "content-satisfied-justified-fulfilled." Their income (and what they buy with it) determines how happy they are. They're always on a quest for "more," so they can't be happy with what they have. It's a great formula for a lifetime of unhappiness.

Begin now to live a principled life. Determine at this moment to live the principle of financial discipline!

Principle 26

The Biblical Principle of Financial Danger

2 Peter 2:19

> *"By what a man is overcome, by this he is enslaved" (NASB).*

This is a danger that comes with being a slave to anything, and money is no exception. You can be a slave to money when you have it in excess and you are still wanting more. Equally as dangerous is when you have no money and have become a slave to a burden of heavy debt. The principle of financial danger is simply this. Do not become a slave to debt. There is serious danger in doing so.

Financial stewardship includes how we handle our money and our debt. Money is very important to us and sustains our livelihood. If spent in the right way, on the right things and in the right places, it can do us a lot of good. But more importantly is the fact that what we are is far more important than what we possess.

Debt is a serious financial and spiritual problem. Usually it means we have slipped into a lifestyle of poor stewardship. Every person must fulfill a fiduciary responsibility. This is a relationship of trust and confidence in our obligation to our family, friends, God and fellow man. Our life's stewardship should reflect God's interest in all He has entrusted to us.

Financial danger comes when you continue to borrow without the means to repay in a timely manner. The only problem with borrowing money is that you have to pay it back. No pressure on a marriage is quite like the burden of debt.

The pressure to repay debt can feel like the powerful tentacles of a giant sea monster pulling you down into the suffocating deep. Robert Frost once said, "A bank is a place where they lend you an umbrella in fair weather and ask for it back when it begins to rain."

Debt is nothing more than borrowing from your future income to buy now what you cannot afford to purchase with your current income. Don't let debt break your back; get a handle on your spending.

Fortunately, potential debt problems can be spotted before they reach the serious stage. By knowing what danger signals to look for, you can take steps to prevent a problem before it occurs.

I have prepared a checklist below. If any of these danger signals look familiar, you may be headed for financial trouble.

Danger Signals of Too Much Debt

- You think of credit as cash, not debt.
- Your debts are greater than your assets.
- You owe more than seven creditors.
- You are an impulsive or compulsive shopper.
- You and your spouse are dishonest with each other about your use of credit.
- You don't know how much your monthly living expenses are or the amount of your total debt.
- Your expected increase in income is already committed to paying off debts.
- You depend on extra income, such as earnings by a second person or overtime by the breadwinner, to help you make ends meet.
- You have less than two month's take-home pay in cash or savings where you can get to it quickly.
- You have to pay back several installment payments that will take more than 12 months to pay off.

- You have more than 15 or 20% of your take-home pay committed to credit payments other than your home mortgage.
- You get behind in utility or rent payments.
- You have to consolidate several loans into one or reduce monthly payments by extending current loans to pay your debts.
- You cannot afford to pay for regular living expenses or credit payments.
- Creditors are sending overdue notices.
- The portion of your income used to pay debts is rising.
- This month's credit balances are larger than last month's.
- You are usually late paying some of your bills.
- You borrow for items you once bought with cash.
- You don't have enough savings to meet expenses for at least three months.
- You don't know how much installment debt you owe and you are afraid to add it up.
- You have borrowed money from a new source to pay off an older, perhaps even overdue, debt.
- You have borrowed money to pay for regular household expenses such as rent, food, clothing, gas or insurance.
- You have reached your credit limits.
- You hurry to the bank on payday to cover checks already written.
- You no longer can contribute to a savings account or have no savings at all.
- You pay bills with money earmarked for other financial obligations.
- You pay minimum amounts or less on your outstanding debt.
- You use a cash advance from one credit card to make payments on others.
- You have applied for more credit cards to increase borrowing.
- You have drawn from savings to pay regular bills.
- Your liquid assets total less than your short-term debt.

. . . and on and on!

This causes you to . . .

a) Take out a loan.
b) Withdraw savings.
c) Skip payments.
d) Pay only the minimum amount due on your charge accounts.

1. If you identified with at least four of the above statements, examine your budget and look for ways to tighten your belt.
2. If you identified with five or more, you are probably headed for financial trouble.
3. If you identified with seven or more, then your financial health is in trouble and you are in financial danger!

At some point or other, most everyone applies for some form of credit, whether it's for a new house, a new car or bank credit cards. Very few people can afford to pay cash for every single purchase.

This is where banks come in. Many businesses will not accept a personal check from a person who does not have a credit card. It is also difficult and sometimes impossible to rent a car without a credit card. The credit card has fast become a major identification tool.

Your credit rating is very important and must be protected at all costs. Whether good or bad, your credit standing is no secret. Whenever you apply for any type of credit you will be investigated. Your payment habits go on file at the credit bureau. Your credit file shows your credit history, income level, and your habits and tendencies with regards to payments. Delinquent entries on your credit report may very well result in denial of credit.

Not only is having credit a necessity, but it's also just as important to maintain a good credit rating. However, each year, millions of well-intentioned people find themselves in financial crunches that severely jeopardize their credit standing.

These are well-meaning people, just like you, who might have been laid off, lost income through illness, and / or hospitalization, job loss, or more commonly, simply overextended themselves. The reasons why you are now in a financial bind are not particularly important at this point. Your aim now is to get out of debt and reestablish your credit.

How can you tell whether or not you have a credit and / or debt problem? Well, you have already seen one long list, but here are a few more:

First of all, ask yourself these questions:

- Are you paying high interest rates?
- Are you being charged late fees?
- Are you getting calls from creditors?
- Can you afford the monthly payments, but not the past due amount?
- Are you making monthly payments, but your balance never seems to go down?
- Do you worry about paying your bills?
- Would reducing your payment help?
- Are you able to only make minimum payments and your balance is not going down but UP, UP, and UP?
- Are you racking up credit card debts faster than you can pay them?
- Do you feel like sinking in quicksand, and you sincerely want to get out of it once and for all?
- Are you always short on cash because you have to cover the past due bills?
- Are you incurring penalties because you cannot meet the minimum payment or are not paying your bills on time?

If you answered "yes" to any of these questions, you have a problem.

Purposely I gave you two opportunities to determine whether or not you have a debt problem. Some of the nicest people have the worst problem handling debt and credit matters, but unfortunately by the time they realize it, it's too late.

Begin now to live a principled life. Determine at this moment to live the principle of financial danger!

Principle 27

The Biblical Principle of Lifestyle Change

"Your servant...did this to change the present situation" (2 Samuel 14:20).

Getting out of debt is an attitude before it is an action. When so many people get into debt so quickly, a mistake usually happens when there is a desire to maintain a certain standard of lifestyle. Sometimes this occurs due to our particular culture of overindulgence and excess, or simply because some young people want to have now everything their parents have, but has taken a lifetime to accumulate. Sometimes to reverse this lifestyle of debt, a change in lifestyle has to occur. The current situation and attitude must change.

What are some of the mistakes families make when managing their finances? Hundreds of wrong choices could be listed, including those that result from making decisions without knowledge or without taking the time to clearly think them through. Some mistakes are the result of character issues such as wrong values, selfishness, irresponsibility and lack of integrity. Other mistakes simply are the result of hastiness, lack of education, wrong priorities and so on.

Some are simply wrong choices made out of greed. How much is enough money? Usually just a little bit more. This kind of thinking gets people into trouble and is an indication that lifestyle changes need to occur.

There are only five things you can do with money. Give it, save it, invest it, lend it and spend it. Notice where spending comes in that lineup: last. Spending should never be the first thing you do with your money. Because the proper management of money is specific and orderly, to short-circuit the system by spending it first results in fiscal disorder and finally financial chaos.

It's not what you make, it's what you spend. Here's a plan for people who have a spending habit that has gotten them into trouble.

Get a plan, get out of debt, stop spending money you don't have and then when you are in complete control of your money, go ahead and start saving for specific needs or for a home. But you first need a plan, a written plan, a budget. A written plan stands firm whether you're on an emotional roller coaster or an even keel. Your attitude toward spending should be "no debt no matter what."

The following is a list of 10 financial principles penned more than 100 years ago by President Abraham Lincoln. I think you will find these truths to be as trustworthy today as when they were written. Part of the beauty of these remarks is that they are short, to the point and easily understood by anyone.

1. You cannot bring about prosperity by discouraging thrift.
2. You cannot help small men by tearing down big men.
3. You cannot strengthen the weak by weakening the strong.
4. You cannot lift the wage earner by pulling down the wage payer.
5. You cannot help the poor man by destroying the rich.
6. You cannot keep out of trouble by spending more than your income.
7. You cannot further the brotherhood of man by inciting class hatred.
8. You cannot establish security on borrowed money.
9. You cannot build character and courage by taking away men's initiative and independence.
10. You cannot help men permanently by doing for them what they could and should do for themselves.

Lifestyle Change Means Doing Without the Nonessentials

In his book, "Who Moved My Cheese?", Dr. Spencer Johnson says,

"When you change what you believe, you change what you do."

You CAN do . . . WITHOUT these things:

- Restaurants
- Movies
- Massages and manicures
- Starbucks and other gourmet drinks
- New clothes / shoes
- Hobby acquisitions and / or expenses
- Lodging expenses at the beach, mountains or other destinations
- Unnecessary vehicles (all new vehicles)
- Cable TV
- Sports events
- Call Waiting, Call Forwarding, Conference Calling
- Cell phones
- At home Internet service (go to your local library instead- it's free!)
- Name-brand clothing and goods such as Steve Madden, Ralph Lauren, MAC, etc.
- Magazine subscriptions
- PDA's and other expensive electronic equipment
- The newest CD's and DVDs (at least wait until they are on sale to buy them)
- Supplies for your pets that are not necessary (toys, name-brand food, etc.)

Lifestyle Change Means Paying with Cash

Albert Einstein noted, "In the middle of difficulty lies opportunity." Yes, it is a huge challenge for those who have been charging most of their lives and are in the habit of pulling out the plastic to pay for goods and services. Plastic–ATM card, debit cards and credit cards–are all stand-ins for money. They are not the real thing, they are just representatives and often poor representations when they often represent debt.

Six reasons to pay cash!

- Paying cash means making some lifestyle changes and sacrifices, but it will keep you from drowning in a sea of red ink on your journey to financial freedom.
- Paying cash keeps you focused.
- Paying cash promotes contentment because it adds meaning and value to the things you do buy.
- Paying cash lets you own things, not merely acquire them.
- Paying cash makes spending difficult and uncomfortable-and that is exactly the way it should be!

Lifestyle Change Means Committing to Godly Principles

Certain principles, if followed, will lead to a peaceful and prosperous life.

Psalms 128:1, 2

> *"Blessings on all who reverence and trust the Lord – on all who obey him! Their reward shall be prosperity and happiness" (TLB).*

You must never keep it all. The first thing you must do when money flows into your life is give some of it away.

You must never spend it all. After tithing your income, always pay yourself before anyone else. Always. Not only must you set aside a portion of all the money you earn, but you have to put that money to work for you. Merely saving is not enough.

God is your source. Your employer, your spouse, your investments, your trust account, your parents or any other entity are not the source of your money. God, who gave you the talents, intelligence and ability to think and work, is the source. Your responsibility is to be a good steward of all that you receive.

Employers, investments, spouses and parents are only the conduits in the delivery system. Taking hold of this truth will bring a sense of peace and calm to your life. No longer will you worry about a drop in the stock market, or the plunging of real estate values. No longer will you lay awake worrying about losing your job.

The way your money is delivered may change radically and frequently, but the source never changes. It is the same yesterday, today and forever.

What you receive is what you deserve. God promises to supply all your needs and He says, if you delight yourself in Him, He will also give you your desires. He is not ignorant of your needs or your desires. He never falls asleep on the job or issues a due date.

All He asks is that you obey His laws and trust His word. Those who do, and go on to demonstrate that they can be trusted with more, are blessed beyond what they deserve or could possibly imagine.

Debt is like cancer. At first it is not life threatening because it involves only a cell or two. But it never stays tiny. It begins to grow and then it takes over. It becomes the master; you become its slave. Never believe that a little debt, manageable as it may seem, is okay. It is not. Neither is a little cancer.

Lifestyle Change Means Learning Some Timely Principles

- A good rule for borrowing is: Never borrow to buy depreciating items.
- Americans are blessed with a lot of cash flowing through our hands. Bring a halt to some of the flow.
- Attack the problem aggressively with a plan. Your credit problems just didn't suddenly appear. It took a lot of steps to get into trouble, and getting out will mean taking as much time, if not more, to draw up a financial recovery plan.
- Debt is incurred because I want something before I have the money to pay for it.
- Debt is nothing more than borrowing from future income to buy now what we cannot afford with current income.
- Getting out of debt is an attitude before it is an action.
- How do you get out of debt? Same as you got into debt– one small step at a time.
- If money isn't working for you, it's working against you – you just don't know it yet.
- If you are not content where you are, you will not be content where you want to go.
- If you don't borrow money, you can't get into debt.
- It's not what you make, it's what you spend.
- Keep track of every penny.
- Make impulse buying difficult. Leave your checkbook and credit cards at home.
- The fear of doing without in the future causes many Christians to rob God's work of the very funds He has provided.
- The only problem with borrowing money is that you have to pay it back.
- The purpose of budgeting is to free you, not confine you.
- We buy things we don't need with money we don't have to impress people we don't like.
- When you find yourself in a hole, the first thing to do is stop digging.

Begin now to live a principled life. Determine at this moment to live the principle of lifestyle change!

Principle 28

The Biblical Principle of Counting the Cost

Luke 14:28-30

> *"But don't begin until you count the cost. For who would begin construction of a building without first getting estimates and then checking to see if he has enough money to pay the bills? Otherwise he might complete only the foundation before running out of funds. And then how everyone would laugh! 'See that fellow there?' they would mock. 'He started that building and ran out of money before it was finished!'" (TLB).*

Counting the cost, or budgeting, is scriptural. Proverbs 27:23 says, "Know well the condition of your flocks, and pay attention to your herds" (NASB). Scriptural guidelines for budgeting can be found throughout God's Word. For instance, if you don't happen to have any herds and flocks, God is probably saying, "Know well the condition of your clothing budget, your housing budget and your food budget."

Like it or not, money is an important part of our lives. While it is true that "money cannot buy happiness," it is also true that when it comes to spending more than we earn, the lack of money can contribute to much unhappiness. If properly managed, money can enhance family relationships and can be a springboard for family discussions that will help the entire family pull together for common goals. Not properly managed, money can potentially become a real curse.

Budgets aren't records of expenses; they are forecasts of expenses. Preparing a meaningful budget (as opposed to a wishful one) depends largely on that first step, keeping accurate records.

Counting the cost will help you become debt free. If your goal is to achieve and maintain a debt-free position and to use your resources in a manner that is right, you need a written budget. Trying to go without one is like trying to find your way out of a wilderness area without a map — you don't know where you are, where you are going or what lies ahead. You might get lucky and get rescued, you might wander around a long time before you get out, or you might not make it out at all.

Even if you have a budget, you still need to review it once or twice a year to make sure your spending habits are on track, to adapt to any significant changes in your life, and to make sure you are achieving the goals you established.

Budgeting will free you, not confine you. God expects us to be participants in planning budgets, not observers. As Proverbs 16:9 says, "The mind of man plans his way, but the Lord directs his steps" (NASB).

Budgeting is a means to count the cost. Budgeting is a tool for managing money. It is a financial plan. A financial plan is a necessary tool in managing money. A financial plan helps in making realistic decisions. Decisions must be made within some kind of framework or design. That framework or design provides guideposts that mark the limitations or boundaries within which the family must operate.

An individual struggling with a load of debt is obviously under more strain than a debt-free person. How many times have you said to yourself, "I need to get out of debt and control my spending?"

Granted, the Bible talks about preplanning in areas of finance, but just how does this help? It helps in this way: budgeting stops unnecessary spending. Do you find yourself constantly pushing yourself or your family to new heights of debt because you want to keep up with the neighbors or your friends? If the answer is yes, you are probably one who shops and buys impulsively, spending money in excess. You probably spend irrationally, and when it comes to special sales at your favorite retail stores, you can always find a reason why you must buy it now.

Budgeting helps you break bad habits. Most of us have taken many years to establish our spending habits, accumulate our debts and dig ourselves into financial holes. Habits are indeed hard to break. It is not so easy or logical that we should be able to snap our fingers and get out of debt, and onto sound financial footing by next week. Not even next month. Not even next year.

How do we get out of debt? Just the way we got into debt — one step at a time. Regardless of your past habits of money mismanagement, a sound plan, carefully thought out, can bring financial success in the future. A budget is simply an organized way to manage your finances.

Counting the cost helps you keep the money you earn. You work hard to earn the money you receive. But, once you have your paycheck in hand, do you use it wisely and efficiently? Without a spending plan it is difficult, if not impossible, to use the money in an efficient, strategic manner.

Without a budget, most of us will just muddle through life, trying very hard to stay one step ahead of our bills. If a budget makes you cringe, just think of the entire process in this way. First of all, you are simply summarizing how you already spend your income and second, you are simply outlining some basic guidelines for your future spending. It becomes your own personal tool to develop awareness of how you are spending, where you are spending, and on what things you are spending your money.

Therefore, as we apply practical concepts in handling our money, God provides godly wisdom. It should free you from worrying about whether the annual insurance payment will be made, whether you put money aside for the taxes on your home, and whether enough money will be available to buy the clothes your children need. If you're not willing to live on a budget, you will not be able to help them live on a budget either. So a budget can be a good teaching tool, as well as a good measure of self-discipline.

Begin now to live a principled life. Determine at this moment to live the principle of counting the cost!

Principle 29

The Biblical Principle of Refusing to Be a Cosigner

Proverbs 17:18

> *"A man lacking in judgment strikes hands in pledge and puts up security for his neighbor."*

Scriptural Insight

This scripture clearly warns us of the danger involved in providing collateral, security or surety for another person. One very quick way of going into debt is by cosigning someone else's loan. People who cosign think they are doing a relative or friend a favor. The potential cost of their signature is usually not explained very carefully to them.

When you cosign a note you are taking on someone else's debt. Rarely do you know just how much and what kind of debt that person may have. Debt is an excess of liabilities over assets. Of course, this means that if you are a cosigner of debt, your assets may be called upon to pay off the debt of another person without assets.

A home, if financed conservatively, may usually be sold for more than is owed by the mortgager. A car, or furniture, or most any depreciating item purchased on time cannot usually be sold for sufficient money to pay off the lender. This is often the kind of debt for which cosigners are asked to be involved.

A better name for cosigning may just be "borrowing a signature" or lending a signature. The concept is really that of "co-borrowing" instead of just cosigning. Cosigning conveys the idea that the action is simply a five-minute exercise of goodwill. Co-borrowing conveys a longer-term relationship!

When you view the action with "co-borrowing" in mind, your signature could actually mean everything you own – your home, bank account, stocks, bonds, possessions, your good name and good credit history.

You Are Loaning the Money

Let me explain what you are doing if you cosign a note. You are loaning the money you borrowed to a person who was too great a risk for the professional lender. You are involving yourself in a business transaction that the expert money manager would not touch.

If the professionals are afraid that the risk is just too great to extend the loan, why would you want to put your personal credit and accumulated assets at risk? It just does not seem like a wise thing to do.

Trusting that the Loan Will Be Paid

You are hoping that your friend or relative will pay back the loan. There's a good chance that it will not happen. When your friend or relative defaults, then you have the "privilege" of paying back the money. My advice is to never cosign a note unless you can afford to give the money away!

Cosigning for Your Children – A Bad Idea

You may argue that you need to cosign a loan for an offspring so that he / she can establish good credit. While it does seem admirable for a parent to help their children get established, think about what your potential action is saying to them. If you are cosigning so they can get their first credit card, you are sending the message that it's okay to buy things on credit that you could not afford to purchase with cash.

You are telling them that when they have no sufficient means to save the money first, then go ahead and plunge into debt. You are sending the message that impulse buying is okay. You are authorizing them to buy now, pay later; pay interest through debt servicing instead of gain interest through savings and investments.

Young adults should understand that it is not wise to go into debt for things that often depreciate rapidly and do not retain their initial value. They should be taught to save first and plan for their spending at a later date.

Young people do not appreciate the value of a dollar, nor have they had the exposure and experience to make wise money decisions. They need to learn and practice the habit of financial discipline. If you offer to cosign for them, they may only learn financial smarts by graduating from the school of hard knocks – and you, as the parent, may learn a hard lesson also.

You Become the Borrower

When you cosign a loan, know that you are now being asked to guarantee the full amount of the debt. The lender has refused to make the loan to the person for whom you are cosigning. His decision has been based on facts that reveal the risk is too great to loan the money to your friend or relative.

Be sure you have plenty of money to pay the loan should your friend default. If the borrower misses a payment, the creditor is going to be looking your way within days. You will have to come up with the funds. You are just as much a borrower as the other party. Do you really want to accept this full responsibility? Be sure you can afford to pay any and all debt payments, and even the full balance of the loan if need be.

When you sign the note, the money is really being loaned to you. The reason you have been asked to sign is that your collateral, your character, your credit and your capacity are sufficient for the loan officer to feel good about the security on the loan. Your signature is the loaner's security.

You Risk Ruining Your Credit Rating

When you cosign a loan, your credit is affected immediately. Does this shock you? You see it doesn't matter that the loan may eventually be paid in full by the initial borrower. Your credit will be affected the minute you sign the paperwork.

How does that happen, you ask? It happens because the loan details get reported to the credit agencies on a regular basis and this goes on your personal credit record also because you are a co-borrower. The federal Equal Credit Opportunity Act requires lenders to report information about co-borrowers equally.

Even if you never have to pay on the loan, your liability for the loan may keep you from obtaining other personal credit that you desire. Lenders will consider the fact of the cosigned loan as part of your accumulated debt responsibility. Because of this, lenders may not extend to you additional credit. This additional debt load you assume as a cosigner weakens your ability to borrow for your own personal needs.

A Vacuum of Information

You may not be notified should the borrower miss a payment. Payment after loan payment may be missed and as a cosigner, you may never know. That is until the loan is in default and the collateral has been repossessed. By that time, it may be too late for you to save your personal credit rating and protect your good name.

Don't assume this involves only vehicle payments. Don't get involved in renting an apartment either. You could not only be liable for rent and utilities payments, but you may also be responsible for any damage deemed to have been done to the living quarters.

Loan Default Consequence

What happens if the person with whom you cosigned a note refuses to pay or misses a payment. In most states in this country, should a friend, relative or acquaintance miss just one payment, the lender can immediately go to you the cosigner and immediately collect from you WITHOUT FIRST looking to the borrower of the money.

The lender may or may not look to the original borrower to get the money. There is a very good chance that they will look first to you, the cosigner of the loan. "Why?" you ask. The reason the original borrower of the money was not credit worthy and represented a great risk to the lender is how you came into the picture in the first place. You, as a cosigner, actually made it happen. You made the loan possible.

The Odds Are Against You

Statistics show that the cosigner winds up paying for nearly three out of four cosigned loans that end up in default. The lender can go directly to the cosigner, bypassing the original applicant immediately. Furthermore, all the typical methods available to the lender for debt collection can be directed solely toward the cosigner. They may include some of all the following: adding late charges, collection costs, legal fees, suing you, garnishing your wages, listing the default on your credit record, etc.

Remember that the cosigner of the loan is really nothing more than a "co-borrower." He assumes all the responsibilities involved in the loan, but instead of receiving the loan, receives nothing. All the risk, but none of the reward!

Asset Repossession

There is always the possibility that what you cosign could be repossessed, leaving you still on the hook for most of the outstanding loan. Ask any credit union or bank how they come out financially when goods are repossessed. Repossession is usually a financial disaster for both the borrower and the lender.

Say, for example, you signed an auto loan in the amount of $25,000. After taxes, licensing, etc., maybe another $1,000 or so comes into play. What if the person with whom you agreed to cosign defaults after just three months?

Assuming you have no extra cash flow to take over the vehicle, and the bank has to foreclose on the loan, what happens now? The bank will simply turn the vehicle over to a third party who will wholesale out the car for perhaps $15,000, and add fees, expenses and other costs onto the balance.

More Than You Thought Is Owed

In the event of loan default, all that extra expense, transaction fees, legal fees, etc., will be added on to your bill as a cosigner. You could increase your debt obligation to nearly $30,000 less the proceeds from the sale of the vehicle. In this scenario, you could easily end up owing nearly $15,000 with no vehicle to show for it. This is how quickly a friendly cosigning gesture of your kindness can turn sour in a heartbeat. Not only would you be liable, but you could also lose any personal assets you have.

Friendship and Relationships

One of the reasons people consider helping a friend or relative is to be a nice person. But ask yourself this. How long is the friendship going to continue if you are always asking whether or not the person has made the loan payment. Even if you don't ask, every time you talk or are together, you will be wondering whether or not he is up to date on his loan payments. When a friend comes to you asking for your signature, why not take the time to pass along the following wisdom to him / her?

Let them know that a good rule for borrowing is this: *never borrow to buy depreciating items*. Such things as new cars, furniture, clothes, appliances, boats and luxury items should not be purchased until cash is available.

Peace of Mind

Are you able to sleep well at night and wake up the next morning fully rested? If so, you might want to ensure that you continue in good health by not cosigning a loan. If you lose the ability to get a good night's rest by helping out a friend, you might consider rethinking what you are about to do. This might be an excellent reason, and reason enough, to turn down a cosigning opportunity.

I Am Determined to Become a Cosigner

While I believe that biblical concepts and practical horse sense suggests strongly that you do not do so, and that cosigning anything is a huge mistake you most likely will regret, if you so insist, here are a few guidelines.

- Be aware that you are borrowing the money.
- Be sure you can afford to repay the loan.
- Before you pledge any of your personal assets to secure the loan, make sure you fully understand the potential consequences.
- Know that you are assuming full responsibility of the entire debt.
- Don't be pressured into cosigning anything without first understanding the full scope of the paperwork.
- Negotiate all terms favorable to you before agreeing to sign.
- Ask for copies of all paperwork, including the loan contract, the Truth-in-Lending Disclosure Statement, and warranties and other important documents.
- Require the lender to provide you with written notification within two weeks if the borrower ever misses a payment or violates any other terms of the contract. Get this lending agreement in writing.

- Ask the lender to provide in writing all the extra costs to you should you end up paying the loan.
- If property is being purchase with the loan, be sure your name is listed on the deed of trust.
- If a vehicle is being purchased with the loan, be sure your name is also listed on the title.
- Be sure the asset is fully insured should something happen to it during the life of the loan. Be sure you obtain proof that the insurance premiums have been paid.
- Once you cosign a loan you are responsible for 100% of the entire loan (not just 50% of it).
- Beware of all the risks involved and take steps to minimize them.

Begin now to live a principled life. Determine at this moment to live the principle of refusing to be a cosigner!

Principle 30

The Biblical Principle of a Good Name

Proverbs 22:1

> *"A good name is more desirable than great riches; to be esteemed is better than silver or gold."*

Proverbs 3:4

> *"Then you will win favor and a good name in the sight of God and man."*

It is biblical to have a good name, an honest report and a history of integrity. This means maintaining a lifestyle that produces uprightness and results in a good credit report. Your good name, in a financial sense, is often reflected in your credit report. It reports how well you have met your financial obligations. Remember that money matters to God because money matters.

Socrates speaks to this issue when he said, "Regard your good name as the richest jewel you can possibly be possessed of – for credit is like fire; when once you have kindled it you may easily preserve it, but if you once extinguish it, you will find it an arduous task to rekindle it again. The way to gain a good reputation is to endeavor to be what you desire to appear."

While I despise the snares of borrowing and credit terms, you do need to know this. Your credit can determine more than whether or not you have a good name. It may determine what type of car you drive (although this rapidly depreciating form of transportation should not be purchased with credit), what you can buy, and even where you can live.

It is important to maintain the best credit report possible. Each person should check his or her credit report and make sure it is correct.

Having a good financial name is about understanding the world of credit. To understand the credit process you first need to understand what information is contained in a credit report. Although the style, format and coding may be different depending on which credit reporting bureau is used, the typical consumer's credit report includes the four following types of information:

Identifying information: includes your name, nicknames, current and previous addresses, Social Security number, date of birth, and current and previous employers. This information comes from any credit application you have completed, and its accuracy depends on your filling out forms clearly, completely and consistently each time you apply for credit.

Credit information: includes specific information about each account, including the date opened, credit limit or loan amount, balance, monthly payment and payment pattern during the past several years. The report also states whether anyone else besides you (i.e., a spouse or cosigner) is responsible for paying the account. This information comes from companies that do business with you.

Public record information: includes federal district bankruptcy records; state and county court records, tax liens and monetary judgments; and, in some states, overdue child support payments. This information comes from public records.

Inquiries: includes the names of those who have obtained a copy of your credit report for any reason. This information comes from the credit reporting agency, and it remains available for as long as two years, as per federal law.

How Is Credit Information Used?

A credit bureau score is one type of credit score. It is calculated from the information on your credit bureau file at the time the information was requested. Consequently, a credit score is like a snapshot: It sums up, at one given point in time, what your past and current credit usage say about your future credit performance.

Credit scoring helps lenders apply one set of rules to everybody. The sophistication of today's models allow for certain behavior patterns. As a result, a 20-year-old's credit history would not be compared to a 45-year-old's credit history. One reason these scoring models are so widely used is that they can differentiate between the credit patterns of individuals.

Only Data Is Analyzed

Scoring models and other tools analyze data only – using this data to predict future credit performance.

A scoring model contains a list of questions and answers, with points given for each answer. Information proven to be predictive of future credit performance is used in a model.

Here are a few examples of what a typical model will (and will not) consider: Information from your credit application such as how long you've lived at your address, what is your job or profession, how much you owe.

It will also consider information pulled from your credit bureau report, such as the number of late payments, the amount of outstanding credit, the amount of credit being used, the amount of time credit has been established. Credit scoring systems do not consider race, religion, gender, marital status, birthplace or current address.

Check Your Credit Report

You can order a copy of your credit report from any one of the three major credit bureaus. If you live in Colorado, Georgia, Maryland, Massachusetts, New Jersey or Vermont, or if you've been denied credit before, you can get one copy free each year.

If you don't live in those states, they'll cost you up to $15 each. It makes sense to check it about once a year, or three to four months prior to the time you know you'll be applying for a major loan, which will give you time to clean it up.

Mistakes Happen

Once you receive it, read it over. Look for accounts that don't belong to you, mistakes made not by you but by your bank or creditors, as well as for any companies that have been looking into your report without your permission.

Report all of them immediately. Once you've found a mistake on one credit bureau's report, you'll need to request the other two and repeat the process to make sure they're all in sync.

Fraudulent Credit Cleaning Companies

Finally, many people want to know if the agencies that promise to clean up your credit rating are legitimate. The answer is a resounding no. What these organizations often practice is fraud – they swap your Social Security number or other identifying details with those of someone with cleaner credit or no credit at all to allow you to start from scratch.

Such schemes also rarely work. It's a harsh fact of life that bankruptcies and other blemishes on your credit report stay there for up to eight years without being erased. What you can do, however, is explain your lapses in good behavior right on your report.

If the credit bureau refuses to remove a mistake on your report, or if you have a good reason (like illness) for your behavior, you can write a 100-word explanation that becomes part of your report.

Lenders who get the full report are likely to take it into account – after all, they're in the business of trying to make as many loans as possible.

Why Do I Have Credit Problems?

Why is it that some lenders say "no" when others say "yes"? Here is why – all lenders make a judgment about

- **character** (your willingness to repay)
- **capacity** (your ability to pay)
- **collateral** (the value of what you are buying)

before deciding whether or not to grant you a fixed loan or line of credit.

Several tools aid lenders in making this judgment, including automated credit or risk scores. In some cases, these scores replace human decision-making. As a result, separate lenders can look at the same loan and view the same credit risk differently.

If your loan application met with "no" at one lender, there may be another lender out there whose credit risk criteria is different. If so, they may have a loan for you. But be prepared to sign on the dotted line for a "higher than usual" interest rate. The more of a risk you present to the lender, the higher the annual interest rate.

What Is "Less Than Perfect" Credit?

How you used your credit in the past and the reasons for your past financial difficulties are two factors that figure in your ability to get a loan. The first step is to understand whether or not you are considered a credit risk. Most lenders will consider you a higher credit risk only if your credit report states you have more late and slow payments than stated in the categories given below:

Revolving credit (i.e., credit cards): No payments 60 days or more past due and no more than two payments 30 days past due.

Installment credit (i.e., car loans): No payments 60 days or more past due and no more than one payment 30 days past due.

Housing debt (i.e., mortgages and rent): No payments past due. This can be proven by providing (borrower's) canceled checks for the past 12 months or a loan-payment history from the mortgage servicer.

In all categories, all late payments must be explained. Contrary to popular belief, good credit does not necessarily mean perfect credit. If your credit reports show any 60 to 90 day late payments you may need to seek out a lender that specializes in less than perfect credit.

Begin now to live a principled life. Determine at this moment to live the principle of a good name!

Summary

Becoming successful at managing your money begins with a commitment to follow biblical principles. In doing so, certain areas of your life must be confronted in an honest, open and accurate manner. You must confront the following areas:

a) spiritual
b) attitudinal
c) habitual
d) practical
e) personal

Addressing only selective areas of your financial life will not bring you to a place of success. You must be willing to tackle each area and come face to face with the clear reality of your past decisions. This means developing a new determination to change past spiritual decisions and the adopting of new biblical attitudes toward the management of your money.

Only you can make a difference in your financial life. You can be successful at managing your money if you will begin to follow these 30 biblical principles.

Source Material

21 Unbreakable Laws of Success, Max Anders, Thomas Nelson, 1996

A Christian Guide to Prosperity; Fries & Taylor, California: Communications Research, 1984

A Look At Stewardship, Word Aflame Publications, 2001

American Savings Education Council (http://www.asec.org)

Anointed For Business, Ed Silvoso, Regal, 2002

Avoiding Common Financial Mistakes, Ron Blue, Navpress, 1991

Baker Encyclopedia of the Bible; Walter Elwell, Michigan: Baker Book House, 1988

Becoming The Best, Barry Popplewell, England: Gower Publishing Company Limited, 1988

Business Proverbs, Steve Marr, Fleming H. Revell, 2001

Cheapskate Monthly, Mary Hunt

Commentary on the Old Testament; Keil Delitzsch, Michigan: Eerdmans Publishing, 1986

Crown Financial Ministries, various publications

Customers As Partners, Chip Bell, Texas: Berrett Koehler Publishers, 1994

Cut Your Bills in Half; Pennsylvania: Rodale Press, Inc., 1989

Debt-Free Living, Larry Burkett, Dimensions, 2001

Die Broke, Stephen M. Pollan & Mark Levine, HarperBusiness, 1997

Double Your Profits, Bob Fifer, Virginia: Lincoln Hall Press, 1993

Eerdmans' Handbook to the Bible, Michigan: William B. Eerdmans Publishing Company, 1987

Eight Steps to Seven Figures, Charles B. Carlson, Double Day, 2000

Everyday Life in Bible Times; Washington DC: National Geographic Society, 1967

Financial Dominion, Norvel Hayes, Harrison House, 1986

Financial Freedom, Larry Burkett, Moody Press, 1991

Financial Freedom, Patrick Clements, VMI Publishers, 2003

Financial Peace, Dave Ramsey, Viking Press, 2003

Financial Self-Defense; Charles Givens, New York: Simon And Schuster, 1990

Flood Stage, Oral Roberts, 1981

Generous Living, Ron Blue, Zondervan, 1997

Get It All Done, Tony and Robbie Fanning, New York:Pennsylvania: Chilton Book, 1979

Getting Out of Debt, Howard Dayton, Tyndale House, 1986

Getting Out of Debt, Mary Stephenson, Fact Sheet 436, University of Maryland Cooperative Extension Service, 1988

Giving and Tithing, Larry Burkett, Moody Press, 1991
God's Plan For Giving, John MacArthur, Jr., Moody Press, 1985
God's Will is Prosperity, Gloria Copeland, Harrison House, 1978
Great People of the Bible and How They Lived; New York: Reader's Digest, 1974
How Others Can Help You Get Out of Debt; Esther M. Maddux, Circular 759-3,
How To Make A Business Plan That Works, Henderson, North Island Sound Limited, 1989
How To Manage Your Money, Larry Burkett, Moody Press, 1999
How to Personally Profit From the Laws of Success, Sterling Sill, NIFP, Inc., 1978
How to Plan for Your Retirement; New York: Corrigan & Kaufman, Longmeadow Press, 1985
Is God Your Source?, Oral Roberts, 1992
It's Not Luck, Eliyahu Goldratt, Great Barrington, MA: The North River Press, 1994
Jesus CEO, Laurie Beth Jones, Hyperion, 1995
John Avanzini Answers Your Questions About Biblical Economics, Harrison House, 1992
Living on Less and Liking It More, Maxine Hancock, Chicago, Illinois: Moody Press, 1976
Making It Happen; Charles Conn, New Jersey: Fleming H. Revell Company, 1981
Master Your Money Or It Will Master You, Arlo E. Moehlenpah, Doing Good Ministries, 1999
Master Your Money; Ron Blue, Tennessee: Thomas Nelson, Inc. 1986
Miracle of Seed Faith, Oral Roberts, 1970
Mississippi State University Extension Service
Money, Possessions, and Eternity, Randy Alcorn, Tyndale House, 2003
More Than Enough, David Ramsey, Penguin Putnam Inc, 2002
Moving the Hand of God, John Avanzini, Harrison House, 1990
Multiplication, Tommy Barnett, Creation House, 1997
NebFacts, Nebraska Cooperative Extension
New York Post
One Up On Wall Street; New York: Peter Lynch, Simon And Schuster, 1989
Personal Finances, Larry Burkett, Moody Press, 1991
Portable MBA in Finance and Accounting; Livingstone, Canada: John Wiley & Sons, Inc., 1992
Principle Centered Leadership, Stephen R. Covey, New York: Summit Books, 1991
Principles of Financial Management, Kolb & DeMong, Texas: Business Publications, Inc., 1988
Rapid Debt Reduction Strategies, John Avanzini, HIS Publishing, 1990
Real Wealth, Wade Cook, Arizona: Regency Books, 1985
See You At The Top, Zig Ziglar, Louisianna: Pelican Publishing Company, 1977
Seed Faith Commentary on the Holy Bible, Oral Roberts, Pinoak Publications, 1975
Sharkproof, Harvey Mackay, New York: HarperCollins Publishers, 1993
Smart Money, Ken and Daria Dolan, New York: Random House, Inc., 1988

Strong's Concordance, Tennessee: Crusade Bible Publishers, Inc.,
Success by Design, Peter Hirsch, Bethany House, 2002
Success is the Quality of your Journey, Jennifer James, New York: Newmarket Press, 1983
Swim with the Sharks Without Being Eaten Alive, Harvey Mackay, William Morrow , 1988
The Almighty and the Dollar; Jim McKeever, Oregon: Omega Publications, 1981
The Challenge, Robert Allen, New York: Simon And Schuster, 1987
The Family Financial Workbook, Larry Burkett, Moody Press, 2002
The Management Methods of Jesus, Bob Briner, Thomas Nelson, 1996
The Millionaire Next Door, Thomas Stanley & William Danko, Pocket Books, 1996
The Money Book for Kids, Nancy Burgeson, Troll Associates,1992
The Money Book for King's Kids; Harold E. Hill, New Jersey: Fleming H. Revell Company, 1984
The Seven Habits of Highly Effective People, Stephen Covey, New York: Simon And Schuster, 1989
The Wealthy Barber, David Chilton, California: Prima Publishing, 1991
Theological Wordbook of the Old Testament, Chicago, Illinois: Moody Press, 1981
Treasury of Courage and Confidence, Norman Vincent Peale, New York: Doubleday & Co., 1970
True Prosperity, Dick Iverson, Bible Temple Publishing, 1993
Trust God For Your Finances, Jack Hartman, Lamplight Publications, 1983
University of Georgia Cooperative Extension Service, 1985
Virginia Cooperative Extension
Webster's Unabridged Dictionary, Dorset & Baber, 1983
What Is an Entrepreneur; David Robinson, MA: Kogan Page Limited, 1990
Word Meanings in the New Testament, Ralph Earle, Michigan: Baker Book House, 1986
Word Pictures in the New Testament; Robertson, Michigan: Baker Book House, 1930
Word Studies in the New Testament; Vincent, New York: Charles Scribner's Sons, 1914
Worth
You Can Be Financially Free, George Fooshee, Jr., 1976, Fleming H. Revell Company.
Your Key to God's Bank, Rex Humbard, 1977
Your Money Counts, Howard, Dayton, Tyndale House, 1997
Your Money Management, MaryAnn Paynter, Circular 1271, University of Illinois Cooperative Extension Service, 1987.
Your Money Matters, Malcolm MacGregor, Bethany Fellowship, Inc., 1977
Your Road to Recovery, Oral Roberts, Oliver Nelson, 1986

Comments On Sources

Over the years I have collected bits and pieces of interesting material, written notes on sermons I've heard, jotted down comments on financial articles I've read, and gathered a lot of great information. It is unfortunate that I didn't record the sources of all of these notes in my earlier years. I gratefully extend my appreciation to the many writers, authors, teachers and pastors from whose articles and sermons I have gleaned much insight.

Rich Brott

Online Resources

American Savings Education Council (http://www.asec.org)
Bloomberg.com (http://www.bloomberg.com)
Bureau of the Public Debt Online (http://www.publicdebt.treas.gov)
BusinessWeek (http://www.businessweek.com)
Charles Schwab & Co., Inc. (http://www.schwab.com)
Consumer Federation of America (http://www.consumerfed.org)
Debt Advice.org (http://www.debtadvice.org)
Federal Reserve System (http://www.federalreserve.gov)
Fidelity Investments (http://www.fidelity.com)
Financial Planning Association (http://www.fpanet.org)
Forbes (www.forbes.com)
Fortune Magazine (http://www.fortune.com)
Generous Giving (http://www.generousgiving.org/)
Investing for Your Future (http://www.investing.rutgers.edu)
Kiplinger Magazine (http://www.kiplinger.com/)
Money Magazine (http://money.cnn.com)
MorningStar (http://www.morningstar.com)
MSN Money (http://moneycentral.msn.com)
Muriel Siebert (http://www.siebertnet.com)
National Center on Education and the Economy (http://www.ncee.org)
National Foundation for Credit Counseling (http://www.nfcc.org)
Quicken (http://www.quicken.com)
Smart Money (http://www.smartmoney.com)
Social Security Online (http://www.ssa.gov)
Standard & Poor's (http://www2.standardandpoors.com)
The Dollar Stretcher, Gary Foreman, (http://www.stretcher.com)
The Vanguard Group (http://flagship.vanguard.com)
U.S. Securities and Exchange Commission (http://www.sec.gov)
Yahoo! Finance (http://finance.yahoo.com)

Magazine Resources

Business Week
Consumer Reports
Forbes
Kiplinger's Personal Finance
Money
Smart Money
US News and World Report

Newspaper Resources

Barrons
Investors Business Daily
USA Today
Wall Street Journal
Washington Times

Additional Resources by Rich Brott

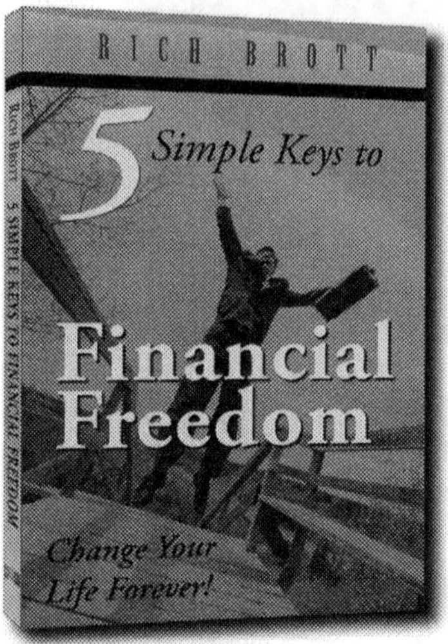

5 Simple Keys to Financial Freedom

Change Your Life Forever!

By Rich Brott

6" x 9", 108 pages
ISBN 1-60185-022-0
ISBN (EAN) 978-1-60185-022-5

Order online at:

www.amazon.com
www.barnesandnoble.com
www.booksamillion.com
www.citychristianpublishing.com
www.walmart.com

www.AbcBookPublishing.com

Additional Resources by Rich Brott

30 Biblical Principles for Managing Your Money

Insights that Will Set You Free!

By Rich Brott

6" x 9", 160 pages
ISBN 1-60185-012-3
ISBN (EAN) 978-1-60185-012-6

Order online at:

www.amazon.com
www.barnesandnoble.com
www.booksamillion.com
www.citychristianpublishing.com
www.walmart.com

www.AbcBookPublishing.com

Additional Resources by Rich Brott

35 Keys to Financial Independence

Finding the Freedom You Seek!

By Rich Brott

6" x 9", 176 pages
ISBN 1-60185-020-4
ISBN (EAN) 978-1-60185-020-1

Order online at:

www.amazon.com
www.barnesandnoble.com
www.booksamillion.com
www.citychristianpublishing.com
www.walmart.com

www.AbcBookPublishing.com

Additional Resources by Rich Brott

Biblical Principles for Becoming Debt Free!

Rescue Your Life and Liberate Your Future!

By Rich Brott & Frank Damazio

7.5" x 10", 320 pages
ISBN 1-886849-85-4
ISBN 978-1-886849-85-3

Order online at:

www.amazon.com
www.barnesandnoble.com
www.booksamillion.com
www.citychristianpublishing.com
www.walmart.com

www.AbcBookPublishing.com

www.ingramcontent.com/pod-product-compliance
Lightning Source LLC
LaVergne TN
LVHW020627100826
845148LV00012B/2078

* 9 7 8 1 6 0 1 8 5 0 1 2 6 *